A Cloud Over the Land

A Cloud Over the Land

The Tragic Story of the Burt Lake Band of Ottawa & Chippewa Indians

Richard A. Wiles

dedication

To the Elders of the Cheboiganing Burt Lake
Band of Ottawa and Chippewa Indians who
have walked on, but have still not forgotten
(Bwa boonendan).

"Pacta sunt servanda"

(Agreements must be kept)

– Hugo de Groot 1625

contents

Prologue

October 15, 1900 — Kerosene

Kerosene is a flammable hydrocarbon liquid once commonly used as fuel. It is typically pale yellow in color with a distinctive pungent, oily smell. By 1860, the main source of kerosene was petroleum. Kerosene is commonly used to start a fire with wood because the ignition temperature is low in comparison to wood. The kerosene oil catches fire first, which causes wood to attain its ignition temperature so that it also catches fire.

I t is early, 5:30 or 6 a.m. on a Monday morning with a sky like cold soot when a dozen city men from Cheboygan take to the road. This assemblage is official and yet also temporary. Ten of the men are on horseback and could be anyone. Not so for the other two who sit on the bench seat of a small buckboard. Sheriff Fred Ming, his face sporting a thick black mustache, and banker John McGinn, in a high-collared overcoat, are easily identifiable should a random traveler happen by.

Recorded history knows these men; or rather, that particular type of recorded history that is set down on paper and then purposely put in a drawer and forgotten. The men are armed. Rifles, ammunition, and boxes of safety matches are on their person. Homemade torches are stashed in the buckboard. Next to the torches are wooden buckets with metal handles and metal spigots filled with kerosene. At 13 cents a gallon, care, but not too much care, was likely taken when loading this combustible liquid. Small spills would be expected. When used as oil for a household lamp, or for an industrial lubricant, or even as a secret accelerant, kerosene is cheap; barely a third the cost of whale oil and somewhat easier to ignite.

The sky threatens snow, or rain, or some kind of weather but no matter. Plans have been made. Checks have been cut. Writs have been signed by a circuit court judge. Today is the day.

For one mile, for five miles, for ten miles and more, the men ride southwest on Petoskey State Road while the coast of Lake Huron, the still-quiet docks, the silent mills, and the rust-colored buildings of downtown Cheboygan recede behind their backs. The posse makes its way through the chill. A greasy stink rises from the back of the buckboard, cleaving the air. Out here in the open, where there are no houses with lamps that need filling, and no mills with gears that need tending, there would be a certain inevitability to the smell of kerosene.

The road turns sharply south, bisecting a landscape of secondary succession. This is lumbering country, or was until recently, and spreading over a vast acreage of clear-cut are new maples and birches sprouting between the stumps of white pine. Most of these stumps are the size of a cooper's best beer keg, but a few are so large they'd make the wheel of a cannon wagon look like a dinner plate.

The men ride on. And whether or not their minds register this fact, they get lucky. Because, while sections of the 20 rutted miles between Cheboygan and Indian Village can sometimes be well traveled, today they see no one.

On the approach to the final portion of their trip, ragged remains of the logging harvest give way to a forest of pine and oak. By now it is after 10 a.m. A slanting light has been throwing their shadows for more than an hour. Ming and McGinn and the rest of the men see occasional vistas of Burt Lake, gleaming through the trees like nature's hand mirror.

They're close now. Close enough to smell the cooking fires of Indian Village and hear the sounds of 23 families going about their morning, though they are, as yet, unseen by those they hear.

The men dismount, grasp reins and harnesses, and lead their horses deep into the woods. They hide the wagon far off the road and, as quietly as they can, find a white pine, or a red oak, or a stand of sumac to crouch behind. And then they wait.

Indian Village is on the southwestern side of a small peninsula, pushing south into Burt Lake like a relaxed thumb. A 1768 map makes note of its location, though the village was actually settled in a distant century. Decades after Sheriff Ming and John McGinn hid in these woods, a 1987 university horticulturist, beavering away at something called eco-regional mapping, will discover pottery shards on the Burt Lake peninsula dating from the 12th century. Meaning, when Native people first began making their homes here, Genghis Khan was a harmless toddler, and the latest technology in Europe was an astounding example of human ingenuity called a windmill.

In October 1900, Indian Village had 19 cabin homes, several barns, a Catholic church, a priest's house, a cemetery, livestock pens, chicken coops, a woodlot, and an orchard with 500 apple trees. Large gardens spread out behind each home, most with several acres of pumpkins, corn, and hay under cultivation. Firewood and kindling would be stacked against a cabin's south-facing wall, along with black ash for baskets and birch bark for decorative boxes. From the cooking fire at the family log home of Peter Moses comes the sound of raw dough connecting with a hot skillet. That is good because today, Peter, 79, is going to need all his strength.

Instead of a one-mile walk to the shingle mill, he and some of his neighbors are going all the way to Cheboygan. Peter's wife, Elisa, 37, kneads lard and flour together, adds some milk, a pinch of salt, and kneads again. She pulls off a section of dough, works it into the shape of an oyster mushroom, and tosses it on the skillet. She will eat too, but not until her husband is fed and well on his way.

In the northeastern part of Michigan Territory there'd once been more lumber camp jobs than men to fill them. One hundred and fifty sawmills, running day and night, helped supply the nation with lumber, fence posts, barrels, wooden bowls, broom handles, and shingles. Tourists showed up to witness this example of industry over nature and to ask if it were true; if the city of Cheboygan really had the biggest pile of sawdust in the world and could they see it? It was and they could. Only two years before, in 1898, 130 million board feet of white pine was sold out of Cheboygan and sent away on trains and boats toward the ravenous jaws of western expansion. It fed those jaws in places like Chicago, St. Louis, Kansas City and other points west.

That was then. By the morning that Peter and his neighbors set out to collect their wages, the forests of Lower Michigan are mostly gone. And with them, the plentiful jobs for day laborers. So when the boss of the Plymouth Shingle Co. told the men of Indian Village to go to the city to pick up their paychecks and that it had to be done on this specific day, the men didn't balk at the strange protocol or the 40-mile round trip.

Following orders, Peter and his neighbors, Moses Hamlin, 71, John Kewehurn, 40, Samuel Kiguguwe, 29, Paul Wason, 38, Enos Cabinaw, 50, and Enos' son, Lewis, 24, simply eat their breakfasts and say goodbye to their families and set out.

It is cold, even for October. The sky looks like rain but the air smells more like snow. The ground is frosty. The quickest route to the city will take them north for a mile or so along the western shore of the Burt Lake peninsula, then another three miles up and around the top of the lake, and finally 16 miles northeast on Petoskey State Road and into the heart of the city. There the wind from Canada will be rolling off Lake Huron and straight down North Main Street. The men have dressed for this in wool coats and muskrat hats. The sun will set just before 7 p.m. and they expect to be gone until after dark. They will have taken the shortest route there and back, and not strayed from it. Which is, of course, the same route Sheriff Ming and John McGinn and their men are taking, except in reverse.

But the men from Indian Village would have had no reason to stifle their voices or hide behind bushes. Maybe they talk amongst themselves about what they are going to buy for their wives and their children. Maybe they tell stories, or make fun of each other. Maybe the younger men walk together up front, the older ones behind.

Sheriff Ming and John McGinn and their men don't walk their horses out of the forest until after Peter and Enos and the rest have passed. And even then, the posse doesn't approach Indian Village until several hours later. A witness account puts their arrival at 2 p.m. in the afternoon. So, what did they do, waiting there with their torches and their rifles in one of the region's only remaining stands of oak and pine?

Maybe they strategize. Maybe they assign certain tasks to this man and to that man. You take a torch. You take a rifle. You steady the horses. But maybe they just want to be absolutely certain the men of Indian Village really have gone for the day, and that they are so far from home now, even if the wind carries the smell all the way to Cheboygan, it will be too late.

Straight, flat and wide, an intentional clearing separates the Indian

Village's two rows of cabins and at 2 p.m., it is into this clearing that the city men ride. McGinn carries an official-looking piece of paper that reads, in part, "This court directed to the sheriff of said County, commanding him that immediately upon receipt thereof, he go to and enter upon all of the several descriptions of land hereinbefore mentioned, and remove therefrom all and every person or persons . . . and place the said petitioner in the full peaceable and quiet possession of the said several descriptions of land."

The sheriff is Fred Ming, 35, and no man of "said County" is better connected than he. Before Ming was elected to the job, he'd been Cheboygan's chief of police, fire chief, a ward supervisor, president of the school board, and even the city's veterinarian.

The "said petitioner" is John McGinn, 61, banker, capitalist, and timber speculator. If it makes money, McGinn wants in. He is a founder of the First National Bank of Cheboygan, and a partner in G.C. Dodd & Co., supplier of groceries, animal feed, and farm implements, a business that has grown so large it occupies the city's "Dodd Block," from State Street to Mackinaw Avenue, and North Main to Huron Street. The man's legend is such that people say he's had a hand in building the Soo Locks.

The "all and every person or persons" McGinn's document referenced are the 23 families of Indian Village. Day laborers, basket makers, farmers, fishermen, Natives of Chippewa and Ottawa descent who call themselves the Cheboiganing Band. In the central clearing, horses jostle their riders. The wagon comes to a stop, and the sheriff opens his mouth and yells something. It may be, "Come out of your houses." It may be, "We are evicting you." More likely it is, "We're taking this land! You good-for-nothings haven't paid one dime in taxes! That ain't right and we're here to collect."

Whatever Ming says, the riders cheer in agreement. Some point their rifles toward the sky and fire round after round into the air. This expression of enthusiasm duly accomplished, the men dismount and move quickly through the village. One kicks in the door of the Moses' home, grabbing Eliza around her waist, dragging her outside, and spinning her to the ground.

In another home, a woman who's given birth only yesterday is resting with her baby. What had been an occasion for joy would instantly become one of terror. In Georgia, in Pennsylvania, in the Ohio country, in villages all along the Missouri River and everywhere in between, a posse of white men like this one have murdered Native infants, always with impunity and sometimes with glee. Yes, this is Michigan, where Ottawa and Chippewa have outwitted Andrew Jackson's removal effort, but the attitudes behind it still linger. Even 70 years later. Even this far north.

From cabin to cabin, the men barge inside, chasing or throwing out anyone they find, then following them out with their stoves, their furniture, their tools, all their blankets, baskets, cooking pots, clothing, and anything else they can carry.

There is no one to stop them, no one to demand an explanation. By now, the men of the Village have arrived in Cheboygan. Maybe they've already cashed their paychecks and are on their way home. The Village's teenagers and older children, many of them boys, are 20 miles in the opposite direction, boarding at Harbor Springs Holy Childhood Indian School. When Ming and McGinn and their men break into the cabins, remove everything inside, and pile it all in a heap, the Cheboiganing Band's women, elders, youngest children, and babies are the only ones at home.

Once the cabins are empty, McGinn retrieves the buckets of kerosene, saturates the floors of the cabins and, right on cue, the posse strike matches to their torches. Indian Village is burned to the ground.

"The Indians, from the old women down to the children, sat and watched the burning of what had been their homes," a reporter for the *Cheboygan Democrat* wrote, "and at last realized the seriousness of the law of the white man."

For the next century and beyond, in dozens of ways and by generations of people, both Native and white, this "law" would be challenged again and again and again. But on October 15, 1900, in Township 35, Range 3 West, eight centuries of Native occupancy go up in flames.

"The little backwoods cabins were actually works of architectural art, and so they had stood through sun and stormy weather as firm and perfect as when built," Ethel Rowan Fasquelle wrote in *When Michigan Was Young.*

Gone now is the fine workmanship of the cabins, built without nails, the tight dovetailed corners keeping out the wind. Gone is each home's artful hardwood accents, carved by hand. Gone is the people's winter food stores, their chicken coops, their firewood, and their basket-making supplies. Gone is the land promised them in two treaties signed by two U.S. Presidents, after the Cheboiganing Band and Michigan's Ottawa and Chippewa ceded 13 million acres of the state to the Government. Gone is the land placed in trust to the Governor of Michigan and his successors in office forever for the Cheboiganing Band.

McGinn spares only the church and log cabin rectory. However, the people of Indian Village will soon not be allowed to worship there, ever again. McGinn will forbid it. This is his land now. He's worked hard all his life. He is retiring and will be building himself and Mrs. McGinn a fine lakeside home, something large, befitting a man of his station. During construction, he needs a place to store his lumber. Afterwards, he needs a pig barn. The church will do just fine. He also has in mind to sell some valuable Burt Lake lakeshore lots to his friends that will help with the house construction costs.

Kerosene, a by-product of coal, does not ignite quickly, an attribute especially true in damp conditions. The posse stays just long enough to watch Indian Village burn. The fire eventually grows so large that smoke from the inferno can be seen and smelled for miles in every direction.

Dusk falls. The men ride off. And as they do, it starts to rain.

When Peter and Enos and the rest of the men return from Cheboygan, it is difficult for them to believe what their eyes are trying to tell them. A place as constant to them as breathing, a place they'd been just that morning when everything was as it should be, has seemingly been wiped from the earth. The first instinct of the younger men is to not leave, but to fight. Some say they are staying. Others say they'll load their rifles.

"No, we won't have any fighting," Peter says. He and Enos are two of the Band's leaders, and the men listen to what Moses says. The people of the Cheboiganing Band do not respond to the burning of their village with violence. They respond with grief, and with practicality, and with memory.

The families gather whatever possessions they can carry and walk to a nearby schoolhouse or to the homes of relatives. The schoolteacher is a well-liked local woman named Irene Train. She teaches Native and white children, first through fourth grade. Between 16 and 40 pupils attend on any given day, depending on several factors outside Train's control; weather, the chores their parents have for them to do at home, the condition of the road to school, and for the children who live furthest away, whether or not a wagon is available and in working order.

Regardless, when they do attend, Train, who's just turned 20, welcomes them inside by ringing a hand bell. She runs a clean and orderly classroom and works to make it as official-looking as she can. In 1899, when she is still a teenager, Irene convinces the school board to purchase a ten-foot American flag to fly over the schoolhouse, an organ for music lessons, and a portrait of George Washington to hang on the wall.

Until she marries a farmer in 1906, and becomes Irene Train Mosser, and trades the classroom for the farmhouse, she will be known as a fierce advocate for her students. In 1972, shortly before she dies, Irene shares her recollections of the Burn-Out aftermath.

"One morning we arrived at school to find the Indians' household goods piled all over the school yard and several of the families making their homes as best they could in tents and crowded in with the one family which lived in a house near the school," she will tell the *Petoskey News-Review*. "The new owner's henchmen, led by the County Sheriff, have driven the Indians out of their homes on the Point, set their possessions outside, poured kerosene on the floors and burned down their houses. Only the church and the log rectory have been spared."

Most of the Band members remain in the area just north of the Burn-Out living in cotton tents or staying with other members who live there. Others erect crude tar-paper shacks to survive the coming bitter winter months. The settlement they all create will become known as Indianville on Indian Road and will eventually contain a new Catholic Church and cemetery. A few members of the Band are said to have traveled farther west, and may have taken refuge with Native communities in Cross Village, Harbor Springs, and Middle Village. Negonee, an 86-year-old Native American woman visiting relatives on Indian Point, may have walked all the way back to her Middle Village home, (a 30-mile journey), reportedly dying shortly after she arrives.

Cheboiganing Band members who live near the abandoned log schoolhouse close to the Indian Village Catholic Church and cemetery are Moses Nangueskwa and Charles Massey. Their homes are the first to be burned, along with Frank Mixsini and Moses Hamlin's home. Twelve days later, in the *Cheboygan Democrat* "Local Lore" column: "The Indians from Burt were in town this week selling baskets. Their tales created great sympathy all over town."

Of equal news value to whoever compiled the column, was menswear retailer P.L. Lapres' window display of fall suits and overcoats, and that a second crop of ripe strawberries were picked at R.J. Taylor's farm, though they were a bit smaller than the summer crop had been.

One

Indian Village Life

The first humans to inhabit the North American continent lived in small bands of nomadic hunter-gatherers who arrived during the last Ice Age, some 15,000 to 20,000 years ago. Modern DNA evidence tells us they came from Asia, most likely by a land bridge that connected the two continents because of low water levels during that glacial period.

Some bands of these First Peoples were following food on the hoof such as large woolly mammoths and mastodons. Some bands of these First Peoples traveled down the Pacific coastline where no ice cover existed towards South America. Other band groups traveled south along the warmer coastline until they were able to turn east into the interior of North America. These First People eventually made their way to the Atlantic Ocean and then traveled north along its coastline into the continent evading the glacier ice sheet in its northern interior.

As the North American interior ice masses melted, these First People ventured farther and farther west towards what had become the five

Great Lakes. It has been found through archaeological study that these groups traveled as small bands of related individuals of usually 50 to 100+ people. This allowed for easy mobility and a simple leadership structure with one individual being the chosen head of the group.

They were hunter-gatherers and soon found the Great Lakes region to be rich in fish and game. Genetic diversity was thought to be achieved by yearly meetings of the various bands where young women and men would intermingle. When the summer months allowed, the growth of the "Three Sisters" crops of maize, squash and beans would be cultivated. These crops had been originally domesticated in Mexico and Central America. They all made their way north as glacial retreat and climate change allowed. What followed in the area of Michigan was a settlement pattern that alternated between small summer farming communities near the mouths of rivers, which proved good for fishing, and smaller groups that spread out to hunt in the winter.

The corn grew tall and provided a "pole" for the beans to grow up and around, and the large squash leaves provided shade that retained moisture and inhibited the growth of weeds. As well, beans, which are "nitrogen fixers," returned nitrogen back into the soil that the corn crops stripped out during growth.

Algonquin-speaking bands became known to the first European explorers and fur trappers in the Upper Great Lakes region as the Ottawa (Odawa) and Chippewa (Ojibwe). These particular bands of First People settled the Tip of Michigan area, at first, only during the summer months. Finally, one band made a permanent settlement, choosing a spot along a large interior lake first referred to as Lake Cheboiganing and later Burt Lake. The term Cheboiganing was given to the spot and the people found there by the first French to visit the interior area of the region. The Europeans believed it to mean "a place of passing through." The small band of First People occupying the spot knew it as "zhiibaa'igan" (an inland passage), and they lived at "neyaashi," the point which reached into the lake creating a small bay. That point of land eventually became Indian Point, and the bay was called Maple Bay due to the large number of maples located on it. The existence of a river, later named the Maple River, was important to the chosen site due to the open water it provided during the winter months.

The settlement became known as Indian Village. At first it consisted of birch bark "wiigiwaams" (wigwams) and birch bark "tipi" (tepee) structures utilizing the plentiful White Birch tree bark prevalent in the area. It was the same material the Ottawa and Ojibwe First People used to create their utilitarian mode of water transportation, the birch bark canoe. The tepee wigwam was conical and shaped by placing long wooden poles (branches) in a tripod shape usually utilizing thirteen hardwood saplings. Large pieces of birch bark would be stripped from standing trees utilizing stone tools made of flakes of chert to cut the sizes needed. Then they would lay them onto the tepee-like frame, starting at the bottom. Often, the weight of the bark alone would keep it in place. However, in windy conditions, the bark would be sewn to the poles using strips of animal hide or cattail leaves or stalks.

The wigwam form of housing would be in a dome-like structure made by utilizing bent-arch frames made of saplings, then covered with large pieces of birch or elm bark. The sapling poles would be anchored into the ground and the sheets of large bark would be layered from bottom to top with sapling poles over top to secure the bark. Mats for the floor would be made of bulrush, cattail or more birch bark. Animal hides would be used for blankets and an animal hide would be hung over the structure's opening. A fire pit would be dug in the center for heat and cooking purposes. The homes at Indian Village were made of these two types of design until 1850.

Life at Indian Village took on a new form after 1850 when log cabins replaced the tepee or wigwam homes. The presence of a sawmill in the area was made possible by the Catholic missionary priest Father Francis Xavier Pierz's efforts. Pierz took up permanent residence at L'Arbre Croche in 1839 visiting Indian Village once a month to offer sermons in the crude village church built by his predecessor, Father Frederic Baraga in 1832. He stayed in the small rectory next to the church. Besides preaching the Christian gospel, Father Pierz promoted gardening and good practices of larger scale agriculture. It is most likely that, by the 1840s, Indian Village residents were already planting the "three sisters" of corn, squash and beans. They were also harvesting maple syrup from Indian Point's prevalent sugar maple trees. It was Father Xavier Pierz who introduced the potato to the area and the growing of grains. Like most other Catholic missionaries, he felt that in order to "civilize" his Anishinaabe flock, they had to practice good agricultural techniques to accompany their skills in hunting, fishing and gathering. He also promoted the building of permanent log home structures by having a saw mill built at Cross Village. This mill supplied large, squared pine logs for building cabins.

However, the Cheboiganing Band members and their "Ogima" (leader) Joseph Kie-she-go-we were hesitant to build the labor intensive structures until they had a greater ownership of the land. In 1836, the federal government had entered into a contract with the Cheboiganing Band and other Anishinaabe in Michigan in a legal document named the Treaty of Washington. One of the negotiated items was that the Band at Indian Village would be part of a 1,000-acre reservation made up of Indian Point on Lake Cheboiganing. By 1846, the government had not followed through with its reservation promise. That led to the Band deciding on an alternative. They would buy back their own ancestral land that they had lived on for over 150 years.

This decision was helped by the prompting of Father Pierz, Michigan House of Representative William Norman McLeod of Mackinac Island, the Federal Office of Indian Affairs' Michigan's Mackinac Indian Agency Superintendent William Richmond, and then-Governor of Michigan John Barry. They all agreed with a plan that they felt would protect Indian Point's Indian Village in perpetuity. The plan was simple — have each family of Indian Village donate a portion of their annual federal government "annuity payments" negotiated by the bands in the 1836 Treaty of Washington. This money, along with the promised 1,000-acre reservation, a school and teacher, agricultural equipment and instructors, blacksmiths, and gunsmiths, also wooden barrels and salt for commercial fishing were all for the land ceded in 1836 by the Michigan bands to the federal government (13.7 million acres).

On October 1, 1845, the acting Federal Indian Agent for northern Michigan, who resided on Mackinac Island, wrote to Mackinac Indian Agency Superintendent William A. Richmond in Detroit concerning $355 being sent to Richmond by Chief Kie-she-go-we of the Cheboiganing Band of Indians.

"Dear Sir: I send you this day three hundred and fifty-five dollars, money left this day by the Chief Kie-she-go-we of the Cheboiganing

Band of Indians for the purpose of purchasing land on or near Cheboiganing Lake for the use of said Band of Indians according to a memorandum taken by you at the time of the payment. I send also a profile and explanation left with me. I have given the Chief a receipt for the money to be applied as above."

The agent, Frederick H. Stevens, stated the money was for use in buying their various Indian Village parcels on Indian Point. On February 2, 1846, the same acting Indian Agent writes to Superintendent Richmond stating, "Kie-she-go-we is very anxious about his land and has inquired many times to know if I have heard from you on the subject. The Indians are very busy putting up houses on the land selected by him. They have perhaps five or six already and one they are working on. They are getting timber for more and they think they will get five or six more done during the winter and spring."

Thus, the $355 in 1845 ($14,000 in 2023 dollars) was used by William Richmond to set in motion the purchase of six adjoining parcels of land on Indian Point that equaled 375 acres. These acres contained the village homes, the Catholic Church and rectory, the farm fields, and the maple tree groves. It was once referred to as the "Idyll of Michigan."

Indian Village residents usually numbered 50 to 100. They were a mixture of Ottawa and Chippewa Anishinaabe families with some being Metis (French and Anishinabee). Indian Point and its surrounding area was rich in game while Lake Cheboiganing, along with its tributary, the Maple River, had an abundance of fish. The peninsula was composed of mixed hardwoods. White pine and sugar maple predominated. In order for gardening to take place, some trees had to be felled. The typical method used prior to the access of metal axes was to girdle the tree and wait for it to die. The trees chosen for this were located on the higher points of the peninsula north and east of the village homes.

Fire was a method used to create a clearing for agricultural fields. Piles of brush and smaller cut trees were placed at the base of the dead girdled larger trees, as well as those not girdled in order to kill the bark. Crops were planted by the villagers in the open areas around the still-standing-but-soon-lifeless sugar maples. The resulting coating of wood ashes was rich in phosphates, lime and potash, which was a natural fertilizer for the "three sisters" crops that were planted.

The 1987 University of Michigan horticultural study of the peninsula revealed that it had been used for agricultural purposes as early as AD 1300. Ceramic pottery shards were discovered along with pre-historic food caching pits. By the 1830s, federal government Indian Agency documents reported that the Cheboiganing Band had at least 30 acres of land under cultivation and another 25 acres cleared for future use. Henry Schoolcraft (Mackinac Indian Agency Superintendent) wrote in a 1838 report:

"The Chippewa cultivate corn and potatoes to a limited extent, but devote most of their time in quest of food in the chase, gathering, or fishing. They also manufacture sugar from the sugar maples . . . The Band exhibits no general improvement or advance in civilization . . . living in bark lodges . . ."

This quickly changed during the 1840s with an increase in Indian Village's population from a census showing 63 in 1836 to 72 individuals in 1847. Also, log homes were being constructed and the agricultural fields greatly increased. This accompanied the purchase of the six parcels of land equaling 375 acres from the Federal General Land Office. The Band felt secure enough to finally build permanent homes on Indian Point.

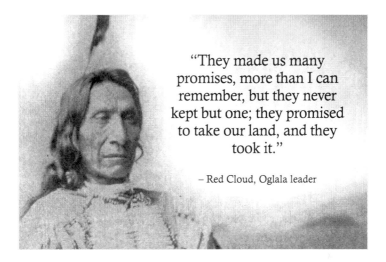

"They made us many promises, more than I can remember, but they never kept but one; they promised to take our land, and they took it."

– Red Cloud, Oglala leader

Two

In Trust Land

The federal government agreed to pay the Anishinabee Bands of Michigan an annual amount of money for 20 years beginning in 1836. It was one of the items the Band's negotiators asked for in the 1836 Treaty of Washington. In addition to annuity payments, the federal government promised the creation of reserved lands, medical services for life, funds for schools, school teachers, along with agricultural equipment and instructors to teach proper use. Items needed for commercial fishing were also promised by the federal government. The Cheboiganing Band was to have 1,000 acres on Indian Point reserved for them in perpetuity.

That legal promise was never kept. No school, or a teacher, or any books were provided until the late 1850s. No agricultural equipment nor instructor was ever in place at Indian Village. Neither was a blacksmith or gunsmith made available other than at the army fort on Mackinac Island. Medical services could only be obtained at the Mackinac Island fort. The first annuity payment from the federal government took place in the fall of 1836 and, for the Indian Village residents of 63, it amounted to a total of $1,444 with each individual receiving $23.

By the early 1800s, the various Anishinaabe Bands of northern Michigan had long-standing ties with the French fur traders and the French Catholic missionaries referred to as the "Black Robes." The French were the first to introduce metal goods to the North American continent. Knives, axes, pots, pans and traps were traded for furs. The French had no interest in clearing forests or creating large settlements. That policy helped the two cultures to co-exist and to mingle. It has been said that the French left behind their metal goods, their Catholic religion and their genes. French-Indian mixtures became known as "Metis" people. No definite evidence exists that the Cheboiganing Band villagers traded with the French, however, it is very likely French canoes passed Indian Point while using the Inland Water Route.

By the year 1800, the political climate in the area of the Mackinac Straits had dramatically changed. Now the British were in charge of the area even though they had been defeated by the Americans during the American Revolution. They refused to give up their forts in the Upper Great Lakes region until forced to do so. Following the War of 1812, the British began a slow movement east into Canada and, by the late 1820s, were no longer on American soil.

Michigan Territory was then ripe for settlement by the many European immigrants coming from the east coast. The federal government already had negotiated treaties for land in the southern part of the territory. When the Erie Canal was finally finished in 1825, the arrival of the white settlers, eager for land, tremendously increased. This happened more in southern Michigan than in the north, however, various bands of northern Michigan and the eastern Upper Peninsula eventually began to feel the same encroachment. They also were in desperate shape economically and many had health issues. The fur trade was now over and the only thing they knew they had that was valuable was their ancestral land. So, leaders decided to cede their lands to the federal government in return for money, health care, schools and teachers, agricultural equipment and commercial fishing items. The items they sought they felt would help them better acculturate to the white man's ways. The bands also wanted to protect their existence in Michigan rather than being forced to migrate west across the Mississippi River as many other Native American groups had been forced to do.

The 1836 Treaty of Washington, negotiated in the nation's capital in March of 1836, included the Cheboiganing Band who were negotiating for their ancestral homeland on Indian Point. The final treaty language included a 1,000-acre reservation on the Indian Point peninsula, however, unbeknownst to the Band and its negotiators, the United States Senate altered the language before ratifying the treaty. The new treaty language stated that the Michigan Anishinaabe Bands would have their reservation land for only five years (until 1841) unless Congress agreed to extend the time. After five years they would have to remove themselves to the west unless that extension was granted. The change in the treaty language made by the Senate infuriated the Band's chief, Chingassimo. He felt betrayed since he had negotiated and signed the original document in Washington D.C. He soon decided to leave the United States and with some of his followers moved to Canada's Manitoulin Island.

Some southern Michigan Potawatomie Bands were forced to move west. Lands out west had no resemblance to the woods and waters of Michigan and many made their way back home.

Under the circumstances of the new 1836 Treaty language, the Cheboiganing Band members who stayed at Indian Point listened to various suggestions on how they might stay in Michigan and retain their ancestral land. These came from the local Catholic priest, Indian agent and state representative. No immediate action was taken and the five-year time limit came and went without any action taken to remove the Band. The Indian Village residents continued to receive their annuity payments every fall. Then, in October of 1845, various Indian Village families decided to pool their payments into a fund totaling $355. The new head man (Ogima) Ki-she-go-we took the purse to Mackinac Island and gave it to the Indian Agent Robert Stuart who issued him a written receipt.

The money was then sent to the federal government's Michigan Mackinac Indian Agency Superintendent William Richmond in Detroit. Thus, the process had begun to secure a permanent residence on the ancestral land of the Cheboiganing Band on Indian Point. The $355 was a down payment on what eventually totaled six parcels of land equaling 375 acres. The first 18.5 acres of land to be registered for a land patent contained Indian Village, the Catholic Church and log rectory, and the adjoining cemetery. The United States General Land Office official register, Benjamin Sherman, at the Ionia, Michigan, land office, recorded the amount of $23.12 as being paid on April 13, 1846. The small 18.5-acre parcel was sold for $1.25 per acre, the going-rate at that time for federal land. Sherman wrote,

"It is hereby certified, That, in pursuance of Law, the Governor of Michigan in trust for the Cheboiganing Indians of who Kie-she-go-we is Chief."

He further wrote "Now Therefore Be it Known, That on presentation of this certificate to the Commissioner of the General Land Office, the said Governor in trust, & the Band, shall be entitled to receive a patent for the Lot above described."

Lot 1, on Indian Point was in Section 29 of Township No. 36 in Range No. Three West and contained shoreline on Lake Cheboiganing, later known as Burt Lake.

Former Michigan State University professor of history now at Stanford University, Dr. Richard White, in a 1980 research paper titled "The Burt Lake Band: An Ethnohistorical Report on the Trust Lands of Indian Village," wrote, "In November of 1844, members of the Burt Lake Band (Cheboiganing Band) went to Mackinac Island to confer with Justin Rice (keeper of the Indian dormitory on the island) to inquire about the possibility of buying the area surrounding their village . . ."

On November 12, Rice then wrote Indian Agent Robert Stuart asking if it was better for an Indian to purchase land in their own name or to unite with others and purchase in the name of their chief? On that same day, Michigan House of Representatives member for Mackinac Island, William Norman McLeod, wrote Stuart to urge the Governor of Michigan to "set aside lands that could not be taken from the Indians . . ."

Dr. White found that Stuart then wrote Father Pierz, the local Catholic missionary in northern Michigan, about his thoughts on the matter. White believes the two men must have come to the conclusion that deeding any purchased land in trust to the Governor of Michigan was the best way to secure title to the Indians. According to White, correspondence shows the main concern of Stuart, Rice, Pierz and McLeod was preventing any loss of the Cheboiganing Band's purchased land through debt actions of any kind, including tax delinquencies. He stated in his research report,

"These men wanted more than just the Band's ownership of the land; they wanted special protection for these purchased lands (375 acres)."

White further stated that the decision to put the purchased lands in trust to the Governor of Michigan, rather than the President of the United States, was quite logical. If government protection was to be permanently secured, who better than the Governor of Michigan and all of his successors in office to act as the future guardian of the Indians within the state of Michigan's boundaries. White also strongly contended that Indian Agent Stuart and Father Pierz, along with state representative McLeod, discussed the subject with then Governor John Barry. Also involved in the decision to place the Cheboiganing Band's purchased land parcels "in trust to the Governor" was Michigan Mackinac Indian Agency Superintendent William Richmond. Dr. White found evidence that Richmond acted as the intermediary in the purchase of the Band's first parcels of land. It is Dr. White's contention that it was actually Richmond who made the first purchases of land in April of 1846 at the Ionia General Land office. These first four parcels of land that were purchased equaled 323 acres and cost the Band a total of $403.75. Following this first land purchase was one in August of 1847 of 71 acres for $88.75, and the last one in January of 1849 of 61 acres for $76.25. Eighty of these acres were patented to a Burt Lake tribal member as an individual. Thus, by January 3, 1849, the Cheboiganing Band, as a group, owned 375 acres of their ancestral land on Indian Point with it all placed "in trust to the Governor of Michigan and his successors in office in perpetuity."

Or so they all thought.

The six official separate registers of land, all purchased from the General Land Office contained the exact same wording.

"To all whom these Presents shall come, Greeting: Whereas The Governor of Michigan in trust for the Cheboygan Indians of whom Kie-she-go-we is Chief has deposited in the General Land Office of the United States a Certificate of the Register of This Land Office at Ionia whereby if appears that full payment has been made by the said Governor of Michigan in trust for the Cheboygan Indians of whom Kie-she-go-we is Chief according to the provisions of the Act of Congress of 24th of April, 1820 . . . Now Know Ye, That the United States of America . . . Do Give and Grant, unto the said Governor of Michigan in trust for the Cheboygan Indians of whom Kie-she-go-we is Chief, and to his successors in office, the said tract of land . . . To Have and to Hold the same together with all the rights, privileges, immunities of whatsoever nature, thereunto belonging unto said Governor of Michigan in Trust for the Cheboygan Indians of whom Kie-she-go-we is Chief and to his successors in office, forever."

It should be noted that prior to being associated with the Federal Office of Indian Affairs Mackinac Indian Agency, Superintendent Richmond had been a clerk at the Ionia, Michigan, General Land Office. This would have meant he was quite familiar in the writing of land register applications and to the use of special wording, such as was done for Kie-she-go-we's Band. When the actual land patents were issued between February 1, 1848, and April 1, 1850, all were written with the same unique wording as the earlier register applications. Land patents No. 5697, 5698, 5699, 5700, 6293 and 7095, for 375 acres of land in sections 28 and 29 of Township 36 North, Range Two West (where the 1836 Treaty of Washington had created, but never produced, a 1,000-acre reservation), all contained the words "in trust to the Governor of Michigan and his successors in office forever for the Cheboygan Indians of whom Kie-she-go-we is chief."

It is Dr. White's conjecture that because the 1,000 acres negotiated for in 1836 never had its section lines surveyed, and thus officially established, the Cheboiganing Band had the legal right to purchase the land listed at the land office as available for "entry" (meaning a transfer of public lands from the U.S. Government to private ownership).

Dr. Charles E. Cleland, Michigan State University professor of Anthropology-emeritus, in his undated paper titled "The Burn-Out at Indian Point," has a differing opinion concerning the "in trust to the Governor of Michigan" land patents. He contends that the land parcels purchased for the Cheboiganing Band were not public lands but rather federal reserved lands already held in trust for the Band as a result of the 1836 Treaty. Its second Article stated, "From the cession aforesaid the tribes reserve for their own use, to be held in common the following tracts for the term of five years from the date of the ratification of this treaty, and no longer; unless the United States shall grant them permission to remain on the said lands for a longer period, namely: . . . one tract of 1,000 acres to be located by Chingassimo, or Big Sail, on the Cheboigan . . ."

At the time of the treaty negotiations, and for a few years after, Chingassimo was the Ogima (chief) for the Cheboiganing Band before

Kie-she-go-we. Dr. Cleland states in his paper "The Governor of Michigan had purchased the state lands which the federal government had no right to sell since the land had never been ceded to the government."

However, by 1846, 10 years after the 1836 Treaty of Washington went into effect, the 1,000 acres reserved for the Band was not proclaimed. So, was it federal reserved land? William Richmond and his successor in 1849, Charles Babcock, both federal government officials, did not seem to think so. They both were involved in the wording of the land patents and both seemed to believe that the wording would legally protect the Band from any type of alienation from its ancestral land, the same ancestral land the Band had agreed to cede to the federal government's General Land Office when they signed the 1836 Treaty.

Dr. White writes in his 1980 paper "The trust status of the land can probably be best summed up as a device of these federal officials who, fearing the fate of those Indians who remained in Michigan (such as the Cheboiganing Band) if a removal policy was pursued by the federal government and jurisdiction fell to the state, sought to guarantee them protection from the loss of their land . . . by making the Governor the trustee . . . In putting this land in trust it is clear that Kie-she-go-we did not act alone."

It should also be noted that the same device was used in 1848 to protect the land of Michigan's Calhoun County Pottawatomie (now the Huron Band of Pottawatomi). William Richmond and Governor John Barry used a slightly altered choice of wording for this small Anishinaabe Band. Their Kalamazoo patent issued on June 1, 1848 read:

"The United States of America, to all to whom these Presents shall come, Greeting: Whereas John S. Barry, Governor of Michigan, and his successors in office forever, in trust for a certain Band of Indians, residents of Calhoun County, Michigan, of which Band of Indians Mog-waw-go is now Chief has deposited in the General Land Office of the United States a certificate of the Register of the Land Office in Kalamazoo, whereby it appears that the full payment has been made by the said John S. Barry, Governor of Michigan, as aforesaid, and to his successors according to the provisions of the Act of Congress of the 24th of April, 1820, Now Know Ye, That the United States of America . . . Do Give and Grant, unto the said John S. Barry Governor as aforesaid, The said tract above described in trust for the Calhoun County Band of Indians of whom Mog-waw-go Chief, and to his successors in office, the said tract of land . . . To Have and to Hold the same together will all the rights, privileges, immunities of whatsoever nature, thereunto belonging unto said John S. Barry, Governor as aforesaid and to his successors in office, forever . . ."

Superintendent William Richmond, the federal government's Office of Indian Affairs head official in Michigan, wrote the specific language "the Governor of Michigan, and his successors in office, forever" to mean the land patents for the two small Anishinaabe Bands in northern and southern Michigan were protected in perpetuity. That was his intent and purpose of the words he used.

In a July 4, 1848, letter to Sault Ste. Marie, Michigan, attorney Peter B. Barbeau, Superintendent Richmond wrote about Barbeau's letter of inquiry dated June 28 concerning Indian purchases of land. Richmond responds by stating in his letter back to Barbeau that ". . . Several purchases have been made by means of contribution from each Band person agreeing to the same and the purchases have been made for the joint benefit and in the name of those making the payment. In some cases, the land has been deeded to the Governor of Michigan in trust for certain Indians . . ."

Clearly, Joseph Kie-she-go-we and his Band members believed that they had solved what they feared most, any alienation from their ancestral land by having it all placed "in trust to the Governor of Michigan and his successors."

They were advised to do so by their priest, their local representative in the Michigan House of Representatives, their federal government Michigan Indian Agency Superintendent, and their own state governor. They now felt they had a long-term home for themselves and their descendants. They began to build permanent houses made of logs. They began using horses and oxen for farming their fields, and they soon would be selling their quill boxes, ash baskets, and maple syrup to the many tourists who stopped by Indian Village's dock on Burt Lake by way of the inland water route steamers.

Life was idyllic for the next 50 years.

Three

A Cloud Upon the Title

In 1855, the federal government negotiated a new treaty with the Anishinaabe Bands of Michigan which included the Cheboiganing Band at Burt Lake. The treaty was signed by most bands in Detroit in the summer of 1855. The Cheboiganing Band refused to do so at that time. Dr. White described the situation:

"Neither the Band's spokesman, As-sa-gon, nor Kie-she-go-we, the chief of the Cheboiganing Band, signed the treaty, however. Instead, the Band detached itself from all other Ottawa, all of whom signed ... As As-sa-gon had said he would during the negotiation, he returned to Indian Village and consulted with the Band. That fall, Mackinac Indian Agency Agent Henry Gilbert met with the Band and a reservation of two townships, adjoining and containing Indian Village, was agreed to. Not until July of 1856 . . . did Kie-she-go-we sign the treaty. The Cheboiganing Band entered the treaty separately from all other Ottawa Bands and agreed to its terms as an independent political unit . . ."

The 1855 Treaty of Detroit designated Townships 35 and 36 of what is now Cheboygan County for the Band members to choose each of what were called "allotment" parcels of land. Many Band members did make a choice, however, these allotments were never patented by the federal government's General Land office. For the next 20 years (1856-1875) the federal government once again failed to carry out its responsibility under the second treaty negotiated with the Michigan Anishinaabe Bands. Finally, in 1875 Congress passed a special act to correct this executive branch of government's failure to act. At that time, some Cheboiganing Band members did receive their 1855 treaty homestead land allotments.

Meanwhile, it was not until 1858, 32 years after signing the 1836 Treaty of Washington, did a school teacher, books and a school building come to Indian Village as had been negotiated in Article Four of that legal document. That fall, federal government teacher John Heaphy had 24 students in his one-room class. In 1862, the Band's Ogima, Joseph Kie-she-go-we, "walked on" and was replaced by Joseph Way-bway-dum. Way-bway-dum was chief for the next 30 years and was replaced by Moses Hamlin in the mid-1890s.

When the Band had its 375 acres placed "in trust to the Governor," Cheboygan County had not yet been officially organized. In fact, from 1840 through 1853, the area containing Indian Village was a part of Wyandot County, which had been created out of the larger and original Michilimackinac County. Cheboygan County was organized in 1853 with the Cheboiganing Band lending its name for the county, and for the river that flowed from Mullet Lake to Lake Huron completing the inland water route from Lake Michigan. From 1853, when the county organized, until 1860, when Burt Township was organized, Indian Village's 375 acres of property were not taxed. The Northwest Land Ordinance of 1785 had allowed for the levying of property taxes, and the county sheriff was in charge of collection. The 1850 Michigan Constitution allowed for both counties and townships, as well as school districts, to fund themselves via a property tax.

No such entity from 1850 through 1860 levied such a tax on the Indian Village's land.

Things became quite confusing for the residents of Indian Village from 1860 through 1878 when a number of elected township or county officials (all European, all white) began declaring their land taxable one year, and then not taxable the next. It depended on who was in office. During this same time period, in other northern Michigan counties, a way to alienate

Anishinabee people from their land was to have the assessor double their amount of taxes owed, as compared to the same land owned by nearby white people, resulting in tax delinquency and forfeiture of the land. By the late 1870s and early 1880s most Anishinaabe land owners had been separated from their land by this device or other unscrupulous methods. Annuity payments from the 1836 Treaty of Washington had stopped in 1855 as stated would happen in the document. Anishinaabe people were now on their own to generate money. Many worked away, which meant they did not farm for subsistence but rather worked in the forest industry as loggers or at sawmills. Some worked with neighboring white folk, or fished for money.

The Cheboiganing Band members on Burt Lake, for almost 50 years after the 1855 Treaty, ranged from a dozen to 30 families on their 375 acres of "in trust" land with other Band members living nearby on their allotted parcels of land. Indian Village consisted of log cabins, a log school house, a log rectory and a wooden St. Mary's Catholic Mission Church with its cemetery. During the 1870s, the taxation of the "in trust" land parcels became more prevalent. In some years, on the advice of John Heaphy, the white school teacher, and other whites, the Band would pay the property tax. In some of those years, the local tax assessor would not even assess the 375 acres nor would the township or county treasurer accept the payments noting the land had an "in trust non-taxable" status; a very confusing situation to be sure. The Catholic priest, Father Edward Jacker, serving the village in the 1870s wrote:

"My host at Indian Village, Joseph Widegowish Way-bway-dum, keeps four horses, five cows, pigs, geese, ducks, chickens and raises feed for them and cereals and potatoes for his family and sells stock to provide for other necessaries including such luxuries as coffee and tea. He plays the organ and reads both English and Ottawa. The dozen families belonging to that settlement built a good-sized church with their own hands. They have a good choir that sings masses in Latin and vespers in Ottawa . . . the proportion of those that read – one teaching the other – by far exceeds those among the Canadians (French) or the Irish (Gaelic) of the older generation. On Sundays, the villagers dress well, even elegantly."

From the 1870s until October of 1900, the Indian Village residents continued to live on their ancestral land on Indian Point at Maple Bay, Burt Lake. They felt secure in knowing that their land was held in trust by the Governor of Michigan, no matter who that might be. A total of 16 governors had come and gone since the last federal land patent with the wording "in trust to the Governor of Michigan and his successors" had been issued. They had built sturdy log homes and had tended to their fields, as well as their maple tree sugar bush. Even when, in 1872, then-Michigan Governor Henry Baldwin received a request from some of the Indian Village residents who had married into one of the other nearby Anishinaabe Bands (and had moved away) and they wanted to sell their portion of the "in trust" land, the answer back to them from the Governor was, no. He refused to dissolve any portion of the trust just as Governor Moses Wiser refused to do so in 1860. From 1870 through 1878, William H. Maultby was Cheboygan County's elected treasurer, and he continually refused to accept any tax payment for the 375 acres of trust land on Indian Point. In 1879 Watts Humphrey became the elected county treasurer and reversed the long-standing practice under Maultby.

He was an attorney and a well-known speculator in the buying of Cheboygan County tax deeds that had become delinquent. In fact, Dr. Richard White found in his 1980 research that Humphry had acquired the delinquent tax deed for a parcel of land next to the Indian Village "in trust" parcels in 1873. He was well aware of the villager's land that had increasing value along the shoreline of Burt Lake. Could it have been that his decision to begin taxing those parcels was personal?

Prior to 1878, the Band's hold on their land had "never been clouded" (any encumbrance such as unpaid taxes that puts a title to property into question). From 1878 on, "a cloud upon their land" began to take place. Cheboygan County began to sell delinquent tax titles of the six "in trust" parcels on a yearly basis. This was done without any of the Cheboiganing Band members being aware it was happening. Their parcels of land being sold for back taxes were only listed in the *Cheboygan Democrat* or *Northern Tribune* newspaper with the owner of the land not being identified or notified, and only a description of the land in legal terms was given. It is highly likely that not even a notice of taxes due was being sent to anyone at Indian Village or to the Governor of Michigan for any of those years from 1878 through 1900. It was a very shameful act and considered by many to also be illegal.

In 1885, according to White's research, after trespassing was noted on the 375 acres, the people at Indian Village began to think something was astray. Resident and grandson of the headman Joseph Way-bway-dum, Enos Kishigo, wrote to Michigan Governor Russell Alger asking their land trustee for help. Alger wrote the register of deeds in Cheboygan County inquiring about what the title for the lands on Indian Point said. He was informed that 375 acres (six parcels) were recorded as being deeded "in trust to the Governor of Michigan and his successors in office, forever." Someone from the Band then wrote local Cheboygan attorney Watts Humphrey for assistance in clarifying their ancestral lands' status. Humphrey wrote a letter to Michigan Governor John Rich on May 27, 1885. Dr. George Cornell, former professor of history, now emeritus, at Michigan State University, wrote in his 1994 research paper, "An Ethnohistorical Report on the Burt Lake Band of Ottawa and Chippewa Indians" (aka The Cheboygan Indians) about the letter. He said Humphrey asked Governor Rich about the "in trust" status.

The letter said "A great many years ago there was deeded to the Governor of the State of Michigan in trust for the Cheboygan Band of Indians certain land on Burt Lake in the County of Cheboygan . . . This land had always been held ever since that time by each Governor of the State in trust for those Indians . . . These lands seem to be covered with tax titles for more than they are worth. There are probably 30 or so families of the old tribe living upon these lands. I believe they have been threatened with ejectment by some tax title sharks who have gotten hold of those tax titles, and they have written to me to see what can be done for them. It does not seem right that these lands should be seized for taxes, they being held in trust for the Indians by the Governor."

This is the same Watts Humphrey who had bought the first tax title on Indian Point next to the Band's land. And, this was the same Watts Humphrey who in 1879, as the new Cheboygan County Treasurer, reversed the decade-old policy of his predecessor of not assessing the "in trust" land. It seemed to make him deceitful. The year 1885 is when the trouble really began for the Cheboiganing Band which has continued for 140 years.

For the next 15 years, the idyllic village on beautiful Burt Lake's Indian Point became increasingly threatened by those who wanted the valuable lakefront property. By 1885 Indian Point had become a stopping point for such inland route steamers as the Topinabee. A dock had been built at the tip of the peninsula and Indian Villagers had created a summer tourist trade selling their wares and maple syrup to the summer visitors. In 1894, the Band had an Anishinaabe friend, Andrew J. Blackbird, of nearby Harbor Springs, write another letter to a Michigan Governor, this time, John Rich. Blackbird expressed the Band's concern that certain timber thieves were illegally harvesting trees on their "in trust lands."

The letter from Blackbird read:

"Can this land, which is held in trust by the Governor of the state, be lawfully assessed for the purpose of collecting taxes thereon? . . . Please inform them as early as possible for they are in great trouble."

The Blackbird letter set into motion a series of actions that could be deemed malfeasance at best, or misfeasance at its worst, by both state and federal officials. What was most troubling was the failure of any official to check the archives of the Office of Indian Affairs in Washington, D.C., for records concerning the "in trust to the Governor of Michigan" land patents issued to both the Cheboiganing Band and the Calhoun Band of Potawatomi in the 1840s. Instead, what first took place was Governor Rich sent Blackbird's letter to the State of Michigan's Land Commissioner William French. Ironically, French had just taken over the office from former Governor John Barry a few months prior. Had Barry still been in office it is likely the whole affair would have ended once and for all. French decided to give the letter to his deputy Burton Parker. Parker could not answer the question so he wrote to the federal government's General Land Office in Washington D.C. asking for clarification.

Parker's letter was addressed to Silas W. Lamoreaux who was the Commissioner of the General Land Office. On May 15, 1894, Lamoreaux responded in a letter stating: ". . . the patents to the land in question had been issued in trust for the Cheboiganing Band of Indians of who Kie-she-go-we is Chief, to the Governor of Michigan and his successors in office in trust for the said Indians . . ."

However, Lamoreaux further wrote what would become the false basis for many subsequent state officials' decisions regarding the "in trust land" on Indian Point. Now one federal official's opinion became the mantra for those not wanting the "in trust land patents" to be honored. Lamoreaux stated:

"It is my opinion, which is coincided with by the Commissioner of

Indian Affairs, in a personal interview, that the individual members of this Band of Indians . . . made up a purse, and purchased the described below lands . . . and in order to protect the interest of all concerned agreed to have the land purchased by and patented to someone in trust for them and they selected the Governor of Michigan as the proper person. While it is not common, it is not an uncommon occurrence, and there is no reason I know of why it should not have been done."

Keep in mind that this was strictly one man's unsubstantiated opinion of the process Richmond and Barry used in putting the 375 acres "in trust" forever.

Lamoreaux did not bother to check his own General Land Office archives, nor did he ask for the archives of the Office of Indian Affairs be checked. This failure to investigate the records on file was outright malfeasance. He had an obligation to check into how the Cheboiganing Band had come to put their purchased parcels of land "in trust." That did not take place and instead officials merely relied on their opinion. Had he and others performed their obligation they would have found, according to Dr. White's exhaustive research that, "The purchase had not been made by a group of Indians short on cash. The purchase had been made with the advice and assistance of the Federal Superintendent of the Mackinac Indian Agency, William Richmond. It had not been made with individual funds, but with the annuities owed the Band. The Indians did not purchase the land to protect the interests of all concerned, but rather as a part of a larger strategy to remain in Michigan and to protect the common land from seizure for debts or taxes."

With Lamoreaux's written answer in hand, Deputy Land Commissioner Parker, back in Michigan, begins to further obfuscate the facts by telling Governor Rich the only reason (his opinion) that the "Governor of Michigan and his successors in office" as trustee were the words used was simply because that way the trustee could always be identified. Parker further erroneously wrote to Rich that:

"The Governor as trustee was not acting in his official capacity for and on behalf of the State. The position of the State with regards to the lands is just as it would be if the patent had run to John Smith or any other person besides the Governor of the State of Michigan."

It was simply Parker's imagination and not based on any factual information. However, it became a convenient excuse for not honoring the "in trust" status of the 375 acres on Indian Point.

In his May 19, 1894, letter to Governor Rich, Parker wrote:

"For the reason, therefore, that the legal title to the land is in the Indians and the trust deed does not vest in the State of Michigan any interest or title . . . I am of the opinion that we cannot maintain action for trespass; and that the lands, not being specially (sic) exempt, are subject to taxation."

May 19, 1894, was the first date that any state official of Michigan rejected the Governor of Michigan's status as trustee and the first state official to support the idea that the 375 acres of land could be taxed. It was a bad omen foreshadowing what was to come.

Dr. Richard White said Burton's letter to Rich was "composed of equal parts of ignorance and imagination." Compounding matters was the 1893 passage in the Michigan legislature of the General Property Tax Act No. 206. "An Act to provide for the assessment of rights and interests, including . . . the levying of taxes on property; and for the collection of taxes levied; making those taxes a lien on the property taxed, establishing and continuing the lien, providing for the sale and forfeiture and conveyance of property delinquent for taxes . . ."

This act was a boon for the tax title speculators known as "tax sharks."

One of Cheboygan County's most notable tax sharks was John Walter McGinn.

The headstone of John W. McGinn   *Fred Ming*

Four

John McGinn, Fred Ming and the Eviction Notice

John Walter McGinn was born in London, Ontario, Canada, on November 2, 1839. The 1860 federal census for Port Huron, Michigan, lists McGinn as living with his parents and working as a raftsman for the lumber industry. It was common practice at that time to tie logs together in the form of a raft and then float them down rivers to sawmills. Those guiding the timber rafts, while standing on top of them, were known as floaters or raftsmen.

By the mid-1860s, he was living in Fond du Lac, Wisconsin, where he married Anna "Annie" Docherty. In 1867 they moved to Cheboygan. At first he was a dealer in lumber for himself, eventually becoming the general superintendent of lumbering operations for the well-known MacArthur Brothers of Cheboygan. In 1882, he became one of the founders of the First National Bank of Cheboygan and its first president. Over the years, he acquired a large amount of real estate beginning with a 40-acre General Land Office patent in the southern part of Cheboygan County in 1876. The 1880 federal census shows the 39-year-old listed as a lumberman living with wife Annie and five children. McGinn was the epitome of a capitalist; a small town "robber baron" type that was quite prevalent in the country during that era. He knew how to make money whether it be in lumber or land speculation. Besides being a banker, he was part owner of one of Cheboygan's largest businesses, the C.G. Dodd Company which was a hardware, harness, farm equipment and grocery store on Main Street.

According to Dr. White's research using the Cheboygan County Tax History Records, McGinn began buying delinquent tax titles at Indian Point in 1882. However, it was not until ten or more years later in 1894 that McGinn began annually purchasing all of the delinquent tax titles of the "in trust lands" around Indian Village except Lot 5 of Section 28. That parcel's delinquent tax titles were being bought since 1873 by Cheboygan attorney Watts Humphrey, a friend of McGinn. It was Watts Humphrey who, as newly elected Cheboygan County Treasurer in 1878, reversed his predecessor's refusal to assess or tax the Indian Point "in trust" lands. What exacerbated the situation even further was the Michigan Legislature's passing of the 1893 General Property Tax Act referred to as the Decree Law. This law changed the way tax titles could be acquired, making it easier to take place. According to Black's Law Dictionary, a tax title is also known as a tax certificate or a tax deed. The official definition is "an instrument issued to a buyer of property as a tax sale which entitles the holder to the property thus purchased if it is not redeemed within a period provided by law (three years)."

If a tax sale did take place, the owners of the property had an additional one year to redeem the property from the tax title purchaser. At the end of that time the purchaser, such as Humphrey or McGinn, could serve notice and/or get a "writ of assistance" to evict the original owners. The 1893 statute also stated that no tax title could be attacked (challenged) after five years.

Thus, beginning in 1894, after over 50+ years of idyllic living on Indian Point in their log homes, the 20 or so Anishinaabe families of Indian Village were under a steadily increasing threat. Dr. White reported in his research paper "In 1895 McGinn began to have the 'in trust' land parcels deeded to him, a practice he continued in 1896, 1897 and 1898. He took no action at this time to evict the Band members . . . until December of 1897 when he served notice upon the Indians of his ownership of the land."

By then, 68-year-old Moses Hamlin was the village's head man, and he wrote a letter on December 11 to then-Michigan Governor Hazen Pingree asking for help.

Here is where a factual "Catch-22" of the case once again takes over. The 1894 opinions of both the federal government official Silas Lamoreaux, perpetuated and added to by Michigan's Deputy Land Commissioner Burton Parker, concerning the status of "in trust to the Governor of Michigan and his successors in office" land patents resurfaced and were used against the Cheboiganing Band. Governor Pingree turned to his Attorney General, Frederick Maynard, for advice on the matter. Maynard simply echoed the inaccurate opinion of Parker that the land parcels were not exempt from taxation. Interestingly enough, during this exact same time period, the Burt Township treasurer, according to county tax records, regarded the 375 acres of land as non-taxable and made no attempt to collect any taxes.

In November of 1896, 31-year-old Frederick (Fred) Roenigk Ming was elected as the Cheboygan County Sheriff. He ran on the county's Republican ticket. Ming had been the Cheboygan town marshal since 1890 when he was only 25 years of age. He was also veterinarian, having graduated from the Toronto Veterinarian College where he attended after his teaching career.

He was known around town as Dr. Ming. When he came to Cheboygan from New York in 1880, he was a 15-year-old orphan. His first job was at Nelson's sawmill, and by the age of 19, had obtained a second grade teaching certificate. Besides being the town marshal, Ming was also the fire chief of Cheboygan before his election as sheriff. He seemed to be quite popular and considered a very up and coming citizen of the county. He was going places and one day would even be Michigan's speaker of its House of Representatives.

One of his most noted features as the county sheriff was his toughness. He was known as the "two-fisted sheriff" who, more than not, never even carried a gun, but rather relied on his fists to control situations. One of his epitaphs would read "Of all the lawmen . . . Sheriff Frederick Ming was the most notorious . . ."

It should be remembered the document that actually set up the territory of Michigan in 1787 was known as the Northwest Ordinance. It was a document based on the writings of Thomas Jefferson and was officially titled "An Ordinance for the Government of the Territory of the United States North West of the River Ohio."

It was adopted by the Confederation Congress on July 13, 1787, two years before the United States Constitution was adopted. The ordinance chartered a government for the Northwest Territory, provided a method for admitting new states to the Union from the territory, and listed a bill of rights guaranteed in the territory including the exclusion of slavery. It stated:

"Be it ordained by the United States in Congress assembled . . . Article Three: 'The utmost good faith shall always be observed towards the Indians; their lands and property shall never be taken from them without their consent; and, in their property, rights, and liberty, they shall never be invaded or disturbed, unless in just and lawful wars authorized by Congress; but laws founded in justice and humanity, shall from time to time be made for preventing wrongs being done to them, and for preserving peace and friendship with them.'"

On Monday, October 15, 1900, that which was prohibited from happening took place in Cheboygan County, Burt Township, on Indian Point at Indian Village.

In January of 1898, John McGinn filed for a writ of assistance, as provided for in the 1893 Michigan General Tax Act, in Cheboygan County's Circuit Court. It was simply a written order issued by the court instructing a law enforcement official, such as the sheriff, to perform the task of aiding McGinn in the takeover of the 375 acres of "in trust land" on Indian Point for which he held tax titles.

Then, on September 12, 1898, McGinn filed with the Cheboygan Circuit Court Judge Oscar Adams an application for a writ of possession. That writ was a legal document from the court which had earlier issued the writ of assistance (Judge Adam's ruling in January) in favor of McGinn to begin eviction. This second writ directed the sheriff to seize the premises (375 acres) of "in trust land" in order that it then be turned over to McGinn. It should be noted that McGinn's attorney, in seeking the writ of assistance, used only certain named Indian Village resident's names. He did not use Michigan's Governor's nor Chief Kie-she-go-we's name, the only ones placed on the original 1848-1859 land patent titles.

According to records found in the United States Justice Department File No. 158012 by Dr. White, one of McGinn's first tactics to gain control of Indian Point property was to recruit some local Cheboygan off-duty soldiers to go to Indian Village and bully the residents off their properties. That tactic did not work. No one agreed to leave their home. Then McGinn, during various times in 1899, led raids on Indian Village threatening and harassing the residents and even having his hired men break into some homes and try to take possession that way. It, too, was unsuccessful.

In December of 1899, a letter was drafted and sent to President William McKinley by some of the Band members. It, once again, reiterated the "in trust to the Governor" status the Band felt it had and asked the President for help. McKinley sent the letter to the Office of Indian Affairs. Again, it seems an act of malfeasance or misfeasance took place because there was no archival check of the Office of Indian Affairs' own records from the 1848-1850 time period the "in trust" patents had been written and issued. Officials in that federal office simply sent the letter to Michigan Governor Hazen Pingree to "solicit information on the exact nature of the trust."

Thus, once again the "Catch-22" scenario that took place in 1895 was repeated. Governor Pingree's office sent the Office of Indian Affairs in Washington, D.C., a copy of Deputy Land Commissioner Burton Parker's 1894 findings that were non-factual and only an opinion. The acting Commissioner of the Office of Indian Affairs, William A. Jones, once again did not bother to ask for an archival check of the records. He simply mailed the Parker report to those Band members who had written President McKinley for help, which was the equivalent of no help at all.

Now, the Indian Village residents sensed they were in deep trouble. No help was coming from federal or state officials who could have and should have done so. A simple Office of Indian Affairs records search would have shown why William Richmond, the federal government's Mackinac Indian Agency head in 1848, and Michigan Governor John Barry had the Cheboiganing Band and the Calhoun County Potawatomi Band land patents specifically written with the "in trust to the Governor of Michigan and his successors in office" wording. If so, the matter would have been taken care of in an official manner.

That not having taken place, on the morning of October 15, 1900, many of the able-bodied men of Indian Village set out for the city of Cheboygan where they had been instructed to come and collect their paychecks for their work in the nearby shingle mill and woods.

It is not known if that was a common practice or simply a one-time ruse to lure these men from their homes. As they headed northeast on their 20-mile trek, Sheriff Fred Ming, armed with the writ of possession, and John McGinn, along with ten armed deputies, left Cheboygan for the task of dispossessing the families at Indian Point. At some point the two groups must have passed each other or, as it has been conjectured, McGinn and Ming with his posse, may have hid in the trees until the Anishinaabe men passed them by.

Dr. Charles Cleland in his undated research paper concerning the Burn-Out wrote:

" . . . they (McGinn and Ming) suddenly swooped down on the village. Cabin doors were kicked in, women and children were dragged crying and screaming from their log homes. A few of the women were able to collect some of their possessions, and with these and their children were herded together by Ming and his men. Quickly, kerosene was poured in and over the buildings as the women and children watched in horror, their homes set to the torch. Ming did not burn the Catholic church (which McGinn would later use as a pig barn) nor its rectory (priest's house). The Indians who lost their homes scattered, their village and their lives in ruin."

It would begin a long journey of disappointments for the Cheboiganing Band.

The United States Census conducted on June 22, 1900, showed 23 families and residences at Indian Village. Lewis Shibwasong was listed as 90 years old and head of his family of two. He was, on that day, the oldest Band member. Nellie Cabinaw, only a few months old, the granddaughter of Enos Cabinaw, Margaret Hamlin, daughter of Eugene, was the same age and so was Catherine, the daughter of John Kewhurn. They were the youngest. The census showed the population of the village to be 74. A total of 49 adults over the age of 15 and 25 children age 15 and under.

Family names besides those above included Boda, Grant, Jonas, Kishigowe, Moses, Massey, Mixsini, Norton, Nangueskwa, Norton, Parkey, Shagobee, Shananquet, Trombley and Wasson.

Five

The 'Good Samaritans'

One year earlier, in October of 1899, the United States Supreme Court had issued a ruling in the Jones vs. Meehan case which involved a Minnesota band of Chippewa Indians. The ruling stated:

"A treaty between the United States and an Indian tribe must be construed not according to the technical meaning of its words to learned lawyers, but in the sense in which they would naturally be understood by the Indians."

The wording used by William Richmond and Governor John Barry was done with the conscious effort to make sure everyone then, and in the future, would know that the 375 acres in Cheboygan County and the 80 acres in Calhoun County, Michigan, were preserved "in trust" forever as ancestral land for the Anishinaabe people residing on those parcels. Both of these Bands at the time in the late 1840s took that wording to mean no alienation due to debts or taxes.

The fire destroyed the village; however, it did not destroy the Cheboiganing Band of Ottawa & Chippewa Indians. That very day,

October 15, 1900, Band members vowed to regain their land. They knew it was "in trust land," it was not taxable, and it was theirs forever. When then-Michigan Governor Hazen Pingree learned about the Burn-Out, he was furious. According to Dr. Cleland's work on the subject, "It seemed obvious to the Governor that the lands, of which he as governor was named trustee, could not be taxed, let alone acquired for taxes."

In December of 1900 Democratic Governor Pingree called for a special session of the Michigan legislature to pass some type of legislation to aid the Cheboiganing Band. The Michigan Senate, controlled by the Republicans, denied his request. The Governor then decreed that he felt the State of Michigan had a moral obligation to restore their land back to them. Pingree in his decree also pointed out that he learned Circuit Court Judge Oscar Adams had stated that had he been made aware of the 1787 Northwest Ordinance's Article Three, known as the "Utmost good faith" clause, he would not have signed McGinn's two writs of assistance and possession.

Besides Governor Pingree acting as a "Good Samaritan," others stepped up before and after the Burn-Out. Harbor Springs summer resident and Fort Wayne, Indiana attorney Samuel R. Alden, had visited Indian Village while traveling on the inland water route by steamer. He bought some of the artwork offered by the Band members during the summer tourist season and had developed an affinity for the Indian Villagers. When he learned of McGinn's petition to secure a writ of assistance in early January of 1898, Alden secured noted Petoskey attorney Benjamin Halstead to file an "answer to the McGinn petition." On January 18, 1898, Halstead's answer stated:

> "In the matter of the application of John W. McGinn for a writ of assistance the respondents to whom was directed a notice of application . . . respectfully show to the Court:
>
> 1. That they are in possession of the lands described in said notice claiming title paramount to that of said John W. McGinn.
>
> 2. That they claim the right to possession of said lands in good faith in their own right.
>
> 3. That the tax deeds under which said John W. McGinn claims to own said lands are each and every one of them void.

4. That these tax deeds are, at best, but prima facie evidence of title in said John W. McGinn.

5. That, as a matter of law, this court has no legal jurisdiction to issue said writ of assistance; there being no legal authority to do so."

This legal action by Alden and Halstead was taken without the Cheboiganing Band's knowledge. It did result in slowing down McGinn's first efforts at eviction. However, McGinn was set on taking the valuable lakefront property and ancestral land from the Cheboiganing Band. He had plans for the fields, maple trees, and shoreline on Burt Lake.

The 1902 Cheboygan County plat book of Burt Township shows he, not only was able to seize the Band's 375 acres of "in trust land," but also took control of almost all parcels of land on Indian Point in Sections 28 and 29. It amounted to more than 600 acres with almost all of the shoreline on Indian Point.

At the southern-most part of the seized land on the shores of Maple Bay he immediately subdivided ten 50-foot lots and sold them to potential cottagers. He was not able to gain control of the 45 acres at the very tip of the peninsula next to his subdivided parcels. That land had never been part of the original 375 "in trust" acres and was first owned by Samuel H. Price through an 1854 General Land Office land patent. It was later sold three times before George Humphrey received the deed to the land in 1893.

It eventually was owned by the wealthy Pittsburgh, Pennsylvania, resident William Reed McCabe, one of the founders of Burt Lake's Pittsburgh's Landings Argonaut Club at Indian River. He and other club members built the Colonial Hotel in 1902. Thus, the name Colonial Point later was substituted for the original Indian Point name.

In early 1903, two years after the Burt Lake Burn-Out took place, Chicago high school principal and Cheboygan summer resident George Armstrong began an effort to pressure the Michigan legislature to finally offer some relief to the Cheboiganing Band. They had failed to do so in December of 1900 at the urging of then-Governor Pingree, who left office and then died in 1901. In a letter to the February 7, 1903, *Cheboygan Democrat* and dated January 23, 1903, Armstrong wrote:

"To the citizens of the State of Michigan.

"I wish to call your attention to the unfortunate condition of a Band of Cheboygan Indians who for

50 years lived upon a tract of 611 acres of land on the shore of Burt Lake, Cheboygan County, Michigan. They purchased the land from the federal government for $1.25 per acre and upon advice of prominent citizens of that vicinity, placed the title in the name of the Governor of the state in trust for them.

"They lived upon the land as a common reservation, tilling as much as desired and building their own cabins . . . they paid no taxes believing they were holding their land as a reservation exempt from tax . . . they were evicted on a cold October day from the cabins in which they had lived for two generations.

"The cabins were burned down. They were obliged to seek shelter from the approaching winter wherever they could. Some lived in cotton tents, some in tar paper cabins rudely constructed, and some lived in a deserted logging camp. Old women and little children suffered with the cold and with starvation during the long winter. Appeals of justice have brought some scoundrels who collected money to help defray the expenses of legal service and then disappeared with the money. Those of us who have undertaken to do something about these unfortunate people find that the only means of relief is through legislation. An appropriation of relief should be asked for, sufficient enough to buy back the land from the present owner, and to help rebuild their cabins and school, A commission should be appointed to see that all matters connected with their lands are properly adjusted and the titles properly protected.

"Can the citizens of Michigan afford to allow this great injustice to stand against these unfortunate children of your state? Will it not cost much more to support them than to place in their hands the means of a livelihood and education, means that were theirs by the right of ownership?

"Will you not interest yourself personally in their behalf by circulating petitions like the enclosed one or write to members of your state legislature on their behalf.

"All petitions should be sent to the Governor before the middle of February.

Yours on behalf of the Cheboygan Indians,
J.E. Armstrong
10688 Prospect Avenue
Chicago, Illinois"

The "Good Samaritan" effort by Armstrong and others caused the Michigan legislature, during its regular June 1903 session, to pass a joint resolution "for the relief of the Cheboygan Band of Indians."

The clerk of the Michigan House of Representatives Charles S. Pierce wrote the legislation that was begun as a "Good Samaritan" act and ended up being extremely detrimental to the Band. Public Act No. 20, passed on June 18, 1903, as Joint Resolution No. 20, contained inaccurate facts that were later used against the Band and the United States Justice Department in its lawsuit against John McGinn. House Clerk Charles Pierce repeated the opinions of 1894 government officials Silas Lamoreaux and Burton Parker; the same opinions, unfortunately, that Governor Pingree used and added to in his December 1900 message to the state legislature before leaving office. The Governor mistakenly said that the "in trust lands" on Indian Point had been allotted to them by the 1855 Treaty of Detroit. That was clearly wrong!

Michigan House of Representatives Clerk Pierce had simply copied Pingree's false statement in the 1903 Joint Resolution. Pierce also added Burton Parker's opinion that the Governor, back in 1846-1848, was not acting in his official capacity for the State when the lands for the Cheboiganing and Potawatomi Bands were placed in trust to him and his successors in office. The Parker opinion concerning how the Cheboiganing Band paid for their 375 acres was also mistakenly repeated. It had been annuity money that was used to buy back their land.

Another very damaging part of Pierce's writing concerned what a federal official, Secretary of the Interior Ethan Hitchcock, wrote. Hitchcock had written, in a January 1900 letter to Governor Pingree, after being asked by Pingree about the status of the Cheboiganing Band, that, "It is not within the powers of this department to afford any relief (to the Cheboiganing Band)."

Once again, as many times previously, that was just an opinion, and no archival record check of the Office of Indian Affairs (of which Hitchcock presided) ever took place — another case of malfeasance or misfeasance of a public official.

Whether or not it was factual was totally ignored by Pierce who incorporated the false opinion into the Joint Resolution No. 20.

"Whereas, the unfortunate situation in which these Indians were placed was called to the attention of the federal government and received in reply the dictum of the Secretary of the Interior that 'it was not within the powers of the department to afford any relief' was received."

While the resolution overall had a negative effect on the Band, one of its provisions was a "Good Samaritan" act. It ended with, "Be it resolved by the Senate and House of Representatives of the State of Michigan, that there is hereby set aside and appropriated from any lands, the title to which is in the State, not to exceed 400 acres, the same to be held in trust by the State, for the benefit and use of said She-boy-gan Band of Indians . . . said lands shall be selected by the Commissioner of the State Land Office after consultation with representatives of said Band of Indians, and with their concurrence and approval . . . such lands shall be exempt from taxes of every kind."

The Cheboiganing (now Burt Lake) Band of Ottawa & Chippewa Indians have yet to select their 1903 Joint Resolution 400-acre parcel of land in Cheboygan County. Circuit Court Judge Oscar Adams who had issued the two writs to John McGinn publicly changed his mind. In December of 1900 he wrote a letter to Governor Pingree just before he delivered his December 31 message to the legislature. In another "Good Samaritan" act, Judge Adams wrote, "Had I been aware of the provision for the Ordinance of 1787, I would have declined to grant judgment to the ouster. I therefore submit this matter to you and recommend that you enact a law providing for the creation of a commission of three persons, whose duty it shall be to secure a re-conveyance to the Indians, or the Governor of Michigan for them, from the present owner of these lands, and I further recommend that the law which you enact exempt these lands from taxation forever."

It was Pingree's successor in office, Aaron Bliss, who called for aid to the Cheboiganing Band. In June of 1903, the Joint Resolution No. 20 answered his call even though it would actually do more harm to the Band than good.

Another "Good Samaritan" gesture took place in June of 1905. The *Petoskey Record* on Wednesday, June 21, 1905, reported on it. It stated, "Some time ago some trespass timber was cut on the lands owned by the Cheboiganing Indians and moneys for it have been recovered by the State of Michigan and the Land Commissioner placed the money in the hands of Chas. Bogardus of Pellston for distribution . . . He desires all members of the Cheboygan Band to meet him at Pellston at 9 o'clock sharp on the morning of July 4, 1905, to finally dispose of this matter and receive their money."

The article also stated that Louie Massey, Albert Shananquet and Moses Hamlin were chosen to confer with Band members to see if the following list of eligible names was correct (people living on the "in trust lands" in the mid-1890s):

"James Shanasige, Thomas Norton, Joseph Benequet, Charles Massey, Mrs. Elizabeth Moses, Henry Massey, Sam Kezegowee, Louis Massey, Jonas Shananquet, Albert Shananquet, Peter Shanasige, John Nongueskwa, Frank Moses, Mrs. Mary Nongueskwa, Jane Grant, Joesph Shebossing, Antoine Shananquet, Mrs. Alice Dashner, Joseph Parkey, Thomas Parkey, William Hamlin, Frank Mixinee, Joseph Norton, John Wanigishik, Lucius Cabinaw, Enos Cabinaw, Eugene Hamlin, Moses C. Hamlin, Paul Wasson, Rosa Burrell, Susan Keshegowee, Moses Nongueskwa."

Many of these same people were living in Indian Village on October 15, 1900. Meanwhile, in March of 1905, the Congress of the United States authorized the Ojibwe (Chippewa) and Ottawa (Odawa) Bands in Michigan to petition the United States Court of Claims to help settle a long-standing dispute over 1836 Treaty of Washington monies being held in trust for them. The Court ruled in favor of the Michigan Bands in March of 1907, however, before any money could be released, a census of the Anishinaabe population had to take place. It was carried out in 1908 by Office of Indian Affairs Special Agent Horace Durant and became commonly known as the Durant Roll.

He came to Cheboygan County and interviewed the "Elders" of the Cheboiganing Band who lived close to their Burt Lake ancestral land, three miles north in what was called Indianville. Durant wrote in his journal concerning the Band "That their village residences had been illegally burned to the ground . . . The center of the Band's long existence in Michigan was in Sections 28 and 29 of Township 36N, Range 3W on Burt Lake."

Band members received their share of the money in August of 1910. It was much-needed. By then, Indianville contained 29 families with a population of 128.

In 1910, a supposed Good Samaritan, who would become a nationally known figure, made his first headline in Wisconsin. James W. Strongheart, who claimed to be a descendant of Sitting Bull of the Dakota Sioux Tribe, got married while in Appleton, Wisconsin. Strongheart had been born in Muskogee, Oklahoma, in 1882 and was a Native American. He was visiting Appleton's nearby Oneida Indian Reservation claiming to be a representative of the Philadelphia-based International Indian Rights Association doing an investigation. He also made the claim that he had graduated from Harvard University in 1896, and while there, was an outstanding football player.

In February of 1911, Strongheart came to Brutus, Michigan, and soon the truth about him was made known. The *Petoskey Record* on February 15, 1911, reported in an article titled "Strongheart, Impostor, Taken by Authorities." He had been arrested in nearby Pellston by a sheriff's deputy on orders from the Department of Indian Services in Washington, D.C. He was charged with posing as an employee for the Indian Service in various states where he misled groups of Indians by telling them he could help them gain access to large tracts of land. He had them advance him the money so he could forward their cause. He was the complete grifter, a total con-man. Before being arrested, he had taken almost $400 from Anishinaabe people in Michigan.

We know that he did talk to the Cheboiganing Band before his arrest. The *Cheboygan Democrat* reported in its February 17, 1911, edition that during the previous week Cheboiganing Band member Paul Wasson had hosted a meeting at his place to hear the grandson of Sitting Bull to deliver a speech. The same newspaper, also on that date, reported Strongheart had been in Cross Village posing as a lawyer and a federal government official. He had been staying with Jonas Shananquet.

His talk concerned the validity of the Cheboiganing Band's land claims at Burt Lake and how he could help. He convinced those in attendance to create a group called the "Progressive Indian Rights Association" which came to an end with his arrest. Before he was taken away by federal marshals, he left behind a three-page letter he had typewritten to George Wickersham, the Attorney General of the United States, asking him for justice at Burt Lake. It is not known if the original letter was ever sent. It may have, and might have had a positive effect on the Attorney General.

What is known is that the Cheboiganing Band continued to pursue efforts to regain their land during the decade beginning on October 16, 1900. No relief had been achieved in those ten years after the possible "Good Samaritan" Strongheart was arrested. This is when Albert Shananquet, on July 20, 1911, wrote another letter to Attorney General Wickersham:

> "Dear Sir
> "We are the Cheboygan Band of Indians, located at Burt Lake Cheboygan Co. Mich. Wishing Heart to Heart. You to tell us . . . About the Land, our homes and propertys. Which we lost, destroyed and Burned, by this John McGinn. Who is now living on our land. This awful happened in the Year of Our Lord 1900. Trusting you will do the Justice and Please answer by return mail.
> Albert Shananquet
>
> "P.S.
> "Please and try to understand each and every word in this letter, that we are saying this to you. Sooner or later you will know that we are the right party.
> Antoine Shawawwanonquet
> Isaac Shawawwanonquet
> Jonas Shawawwanonquet
> Moses Nongueskwa
> Paul Wasson
> If you wish we will give or sign more names next time. A.S."

This letter seemed to have moved Attorney General Wickersham to action and he became a Good Samaritan. In June of 1911, the United States Department of Justice headed by the Attorney General, initiated a federal lawsuit against John McGinn.

Forced from their home ...

George Catlin Big Sail, Ogima (Chief) of the Cheboiganing Band 1800-1839, who signed the 1836 Treaty of Washington

A farming field

Francis, Charles and Sara Massey

Charles Massey (Henry's father)

Road leading from church to Burt Lake at "Colonial Point" prior to the burn-out in 1900. My father (Henry J. Massey) was 12 years old when they were burned out. His mother was Sara Mongreshkrva and father Charles Massey

— Mary Margaret Swartout, Pellston

The Massey family

ABOVE: Mose Bwanishing (Wabwadum), Jane Jane Wasso, Mary Boda, Elizabeth Nangeshkwa, Susan Shenankwat, Samuel and Thomas Parkey, Louise Wasso, Steven B. Moses, Charles P., John B., William B., Edmond P., Susan Shenonquet, Ellen P., Agnes Bwanishing.

ABOVE, RIGHT: Alfons Boda, Joe Massey (son of Henry Jr), and Francis Boda

RIGHT: Picture taken in Burt Lake outside of the Reservation 1900. From left, Joe Paki, Sam Kijigo, Mrs. Liza Nangeskwa, Mose Nangeskwa, John Nangeskwa

Parts of three families pictured here were forced to abandon their homes in Burt Lake, prodded by the armed deputies of Cheboygan County —

Back row: Albert Shenonquet, Mrs. Albert Shenonquet (Liza Dagamking),
Frank Shenonquet (uncle)
Front row: Antwine Shenonquet (Albert's grandfather), Cora Shenonquet (Albert's daughter),
Mrs. Antwine Shenonquet (Albert's grandmother) and Josephine Shenoskey.

Quill box made by a Burt
Lake band member

Albert Shananquet
at topinabee in 1956

Moses Hamelin, middle left with pole on his shoulder in the 1890s

Pictured in this photo are: Maude Dashner, Hattie Hamelin, Jane Grant (Wasson), Rose Shenoskey, Mrs. Tom Norton (Josette), John Dashner, Mary Cabinaw, Alice Dashner, Enos Cabinaw, Sam Shenonquet, Joe Grant, Joe Paki, Charles Massey, John Nongeshkwa, James Shenoskey, Alex Kodash, Ed Paki, Frank Mixeney, Tom Norton (on buggy), Maggie Hamelin (seated), Barbara Shenoskey, Charles Paki, John Dashner

School house Burt Lake

Enos and Mary Cabinaw

"Old cemetery - church Near Lathers Farm. People burned out"

The cemetery as seen in 1983

The Colonial Hotel, Burt Lake, Michigan

This is the farm home that John W. McGinn built on the property after the Burn-Out. It was the caretaker's home on Chickagami Trail.

This garage was a church of the old Burt Lake Indian Village. McGinn first used it as his pig barn.

Joseph Howell, special agent sent by Office of Indian Affairs in 1914 to investigate claims after the Burn-Out.

B U R T   L A K E

23   26   35

21

Equannal Point

28   33

John Chas Johnson

T. B. Renzor Lima

J. B. Chas Bellant

John W. McGinns

29   32

Thos Burtell

R. M. Johnson

Plymouth Shingle Co

Abby White   State Swamp

E. Oobenan Grapes

State Swamp Land   80

L. Mianero

Mary McDonald   W. & E. Franklin

Benham Longyear   G. C. Fitch

T. D.   State Swamp

Jos. Parkey

J. B. McArthur

19   30   31

E. Nixon Residence

P. McArthur   B. S. Widman

U. S. Government

S. H. Maple   H. Ontonagon

Chandler

M.

Louis Sebastian

J. H. Mayott

Swamp

59

Copy of the original June 1848 General Land Office patent issued on behalf of the Cheboiganing Band of Ottawa & Chippewa Indians. It was first of six patents issued between 1848 and 1850. Each one read:

"WHEREAS the Governor of Michigan and his successors in office in Trust for the Sheboygan Indians of whom Kie-she-go-we in Chief . . . to have and to hold . . . forever."

Lo, the Poor Indian

Six

An Era of Bigotry

The years of the late 19th and early 20th centuries in the United States were times of heightened prejudice and racism. White Anglo-Americans felt threatened by the increasing hordes of European immigrants and that fear aided the negative feelings in this country against Black Americans, Asian Americans, and Native Americans. The Burt Lake Burn-Out was a product of those times and those negative feelings were combined with greed.

One of the racist terms used towards Native Americans at the turn of the century was to refer to them as "Lo," "Mr. Lo," or "Mrs. Lo." It was a derogatory slang derived from the Alexander Pope poem of 1730, "Lo, the Poor Indian."

The *Cheboygan Democrat* newspaper on October 20, 1900, five days after the destruction of Indian Village, mentioned the Burn-Out this way:

"LO! THE POOR INDIAN — His Untutored Mind Gets A Shock. He is Fired Out at Indian Village and the Place Burned.

"What the future of the Indians will be, cannot at present be told, they have long been a charge on the County to a more or less extent for years, and it is probable that will become more of a burden now that they are homeless."

That was the extent of the local white sympathy publicly expressed at the time. In 1900, and all the years prior, the sentiment toward the nation's First People and for the Michigan Anishinaabe had been disdainful. One of the worst examples of that disdain was the Wounded Knee massacre that took place on December 29, 1890, ten years prior to the October 15, 1900 Burn-Out. On that day, the United States Army cavalry rode into the Lakota Sioux Pine Ridge Reservation village and by the time the raid was over, 250 men, women, and children at that village were killed. Some claim the number was as high as 300 Lakota who were killed that day. The army lost 30 soldiers. The Medal of Honor was later awarded to 20 of the soldiers who participated in the massacre.

At the end of the American Civil War, the United States federal government began to send its soldiers west of the Mississippi River to force Native Americans to assimilate into the American population. If they did not, they were forced to live on government-designated reservations such as Pine Ridge Reservation in South Dakota. History shows that Indian Wars that began in 1865 continued in the western United States after Wounded Knee and after the Burt Lake Burn-Out.

In fact, it was not until late 1924 when the last armed conflict in this country between Native Americans and the United States military took place in Arizona. The same year, the June 2, 1924 Indian Citizenship Act was passed by Congress giving citizenship to all indigenous people of the United States. While the 14th Amendment to the Constitution, which went into effect in 1868, had granted citizenship rights to any and all people born in this country, the overt prejudice and racism by Congress and the nation's courts interpreted the amendment did not apply to the Native Americans of this country. How ironic, to say the least.

The first immigrants to arrive in North America and what later became the United States were the last to be granted citizenship, 24 years after the Burt Lake Burn-Out.

While nationally the overt prejudice, bigotry and racism towards Native Americans persisted almost from the time of the white European arrival in the early 1600s, it was even more pronounced in the Upper Great Lakes Region, especially northern Michigan.

The War of 1812, between Great Britain, Canada and the United States was mostly fought along the border with Canada. Battles took place on both sides of Lake Erie and Lake Ontario. Many Michigan Territory Ottawa, Ojibwe and Potawatomi Bands participated in the battles of the war on the side of the British. They did so thinking they were protecting their Indian Territory (Reserve) set up for them prior to the American Revolution by the British government.

Hatred by the white settlers in the Michigan Territory towards Anishinaabe People after the war ended was fierce. An outgrowth of that hatred was seen in Wisconsin in 1832 when the United States Army clashed with the Sauk, Fox and Potawatomi Bands of Illinois and Wisconsin area led by Black Hawk. The war was over land, however, Black Hawk and many of his followers had fought for the British in the War of 1812 and that involvement heightened feelings among the white settlers of the area.

An example of the hostile feelings and racial bigotry practiced against the Indigenous People of this country was the Indian Removal Act passed by Congress in 1830 with the backing of then-President Andrew Jackson. The Act legally deprived Indian tribes of the right to live in the eastern United States, forcing some 100,000 Indians to move to the west of the Mississippi River from their ancestral land. Southern Michigan Territory residing Potawatomi Bands were part of this group forced to leave.

The 1836 Treaty of Washington was not ratified by Congress until it contained language (not discussed during negotiations with Cheboiganing Band members or other Michigan Territory Bands) solely written by a few Senators. The rewritten Article Two stated, "From the cession aforesaid the tribes reserve for their own use, to be held in common the following tracts for the term of five years from the date of the ratification of this treaty, and no longer; unless the United States shall grant them permission to remain on the said lands for a longer period."

The Senators who demanded this language wanted them all gone from the eastern United States and territories. This Act had consequences for the Cheboiganing Band whose members did not want to move from their ancestral land at Indian Village. Some even left for Canada.

Ironically, the one Anishinaabe Band of northern Michigan who did not participate in the American Revolution on the side of the British, nor in the War of 1812 on the side of the British, was the Cheboiganing Band of Ottawa and Chippewa at Indian Village. They never participated in armed conflict until the American Civil War when six Band members voluntarily joined the Union Army and two of them became members of the famed Michigan Company K sharpshooters. The Civil War Band members included Simon Keji-Kowe who was wounded, Moses Hamlin and Joseph Wabwetum. After the Burn-Out some Band members joined the U.S. Army in World War I and World War II. These included Samuel Shananquet, Edmund Parkey, Patrick Nongueshkwa and Nicholas Naganashe. Nongueshkwa and Naganashe were both killed in action during World War II. Other World War II participants and Band members whose family had been burned out included Francis Moses, Frederick Kishego, Edward and Harry Shenoskey, and Samuel Parkey. During the Korean War and Vietnam War, two Parkeys, a Shananquet, and a Shenoskey served this country.

Author and historian J.D.C. Atkins in his article, "Americanizing the American Indian States," wrote "Although more than 300 Native languages existed in what is now the continental United States, as different from each other as Turkish, English, and Chinese, that number greatly diminished in the aftermath of European colonization. Indigenous population loss through disease and war exacted a toll as did ongoing measures to Europeanize and Christianize Native people at the expense of their own cultures and languages. Dialect should be blotted out and the English language substituted."

"Being an Indian" could not be tolerated. They had to be changed into being "White."

If one needs an example of the presence of extreme racism by whites towards the Michigan Anishinaabe, the Indian boarding schools that were created in the 1880s is such. Boarding schools for Native children, often run by Christian organizations, such as the Harbor Springs Holy Childhood of Jesus School, were created to remove Native identities. Richard Pratt, superintendent of the Carlisle Indian Boarding School in Pennsylvania stated in a speech the boarding school philosophy was to "Kill the Indian, and save the man." All boarding schools set out to "civilize" or "Americanize" their Native students.

Native children were required to cut their hair, wear uniforms, speak only English, and take Anglicized names. For over 100 years until 1978, Native children could legally be kidnapped from their families by the U.S. government and forced to attend these boarding schools. During much of our nation's history, the federal government outlawed Native American religious practices as well. What other group of people in the history of the United States had that happen to them?

Historians like to talk about "presentism" when writing about the past. This is the idea that using present day attitudes, values and concepts to interpret the past is fallacious thinking and an example of cultural bias. It can lead to a distorted and untrue view of the past. Should we judge people of the past using morals of today? Simply stated, presentism is a method of projecting our ideas into the past. This happens when one writes about historical events from a modern viewpoint. Looking back at the prejudice, racism and bigotry exercised against the Anishinaabe People here in northern Michigan during the late 19th into the 20th century (and beyond), using today's values and insights can actually help one better understand the feelings toward the Cheboiganing Band at Indian Village.

Dr. Dennis Albert, visiting professor of horticulture at the University of Michigan's Bio-Station on Douglas Lake, and Dr. Leah Minc did research on Indian Point for a paper in 1987 titled "The Natural Ecology and Cultural History of Indian (Colonial) Point Red Oak Stands."

In their joint field research, Albert and Minc found ancient caching pits where food such as corn was stored. Inside some caches were shards of ceramic pots that dated back to 1300-1500 A.D. These pits showed Indian Point was inhabited by Anishinaabe ancestors at least 400 to 600 years before the Burn-Out. In their search of Cheboygan County land records, Albert and Minc found that it did not take John McGinn long before he started to cash in on the land value of the Burt Lake shoreline on Indian Point.

By 1900, it was clear that all of northwestern Michigan in the lower peninsula, from Charlevoix to Petoskey, to Harbor Springs, to Burt Lake and Mullet Lake on north to Mackinac Island, was a destination summer paradise for the midwest's wealthy.

Real estate was now being valued not for its lumbering potential, much of that was already gone, it was being highly valuable for its possible summer resort potential. No peninsula in the area other than Harbor Point was more potentially sought-after than Burt Lake's Indian Point.

By 1902, McGinn's holdings had increased, from the 375 acres at Indian Village grabbed by him in October of 1900, to almost double that. Through outright purchase of real estate to buying more tax titles, McGinn became the largest land owner of the peninsula. During 1901 he began to subdivide the southern point of his property. He did not own and could not get title to the furthest 45 acres of land at the very tip of the peninsula. That highly valuable piece of property (never part of the 375 acres of "in trust" land) had been secured by a group of wealthy businessmen from Pittsburgh with the idea of building a luxurious 75-room hotel. It was completed in time for the 1902 summer season and was three stories in height. They named it the Colonial. It would exist for the next seven summers before burning to the ground in 1909. It was never rebuilt.

During the early years of 1900, rumor had it that the Grand Rapids & Indiana Railway had decided to build a spur east from Brutus to Indian Point to service the many new cottages and the new hotel. That did not take place, however, McGinn did begin to subdivide his most valuable property seized from the Cheboiganing Band. He sold 50-foot shoreline lots from the property line of the Colonial Hotel northwest toward his farmhouse cottage constructed in 1901.

He had sold six of the first ten lots as shown in the 1902 Cheboygan County plat book. The new property owners on the Band's old ancestral land included Anderson, Indiana, banker Carroll K. McCullough and Burton H. Gedge, of the same city, who owned the Gedge Brothers Iron Roofing Company. His company would put the new iron roof on the Colonial Hotel. Another new landowner on Indian Point was Charles L. Henry of Anderson and Indianapolis, Indiana. He owned the When Clothing Company in those two towns. Lewis A. Cornwell purchased a lot. He was the head of the Cornwell Beef Company in Saginaw and had vast interests in lumbering in Cheboygan County. One of the purchasers of the Band's land owned two lots next to one another, Richard T. Brennan, a railroad man from Cincinnati, Ohio.

The *Cheboygan Democrat,* in its April 27, 1901, edition, contained a short article about West Burt Township. It read:

"The inhabitants of West Burt are likely to see farming operations conducted on a much more extensive scale than they have been accustomed to. Five heavy teams, mostly loaded with seed were driven on Saturday to what was recently called Indian Village but now renamed McGinn Town in derision, there being now only one dwelling house, a church and small cemetery."

Through an illegal and immoral land-grab, McGinn acquired cleared fields, a sugar bush, a road, fences, apple trees and three Anishinaabe burial grounds, one Christian, the others pre-Christian. Eventually, the Catholic Church built in 1883 was turned into his pig barn. By the 1905 summer season, the name Colonial Point had replaced Indian Point for which the peninsula had been previously called for over 100 years, just like the name, Lake Cheboiganing, had been replaced by Burt Lake. All references to the ancestral land of the Cheboiganing Band were being erased from history. The May 2, 1902, *Cheboygan Democrat* carried a small item that stated:

"A large force of laborers and mechanics are being employed at both new summer resorts on Indian Point, Burt Lake. Rapid improvements are being made. When they are completed, they will be lovely resting places."

Most likely this was referring to the McGinn property and further south on the peninsula where the building of the Colonial Hotel was taking place.

McGinn had his large farm summer cottage on the shoreline built during the 1901 season. He also had barns erected and stumps in the fields dynamited so he could use the old Indian fields for his own agricultural purposes. Meanwhile, the Band members burned out of their homes and fields were forced to find a new place to live. Dr. Alice Littlefield, professor of sociology emeritus at Central Michigan University, found in her 2005 research concerning the Burn-Out, that:

"Many of the members of the Burt Lake Band moved from Indian Point to Indian Road and the surrounding area. Having no money and no place to live, they were granted housing on the property of those Band members who already resided on or near what they refer to as Indian Trail. Local land records show a number of homes being built on the Nonqueskwa and Massey homesteads."

Dr. Littlefield's research found that the core of the community was reconstituted on Indian Road, just three miles north of Indian Village. By 1908 a new Catholic Church was built on property donated by some Band members. While the June 1900 federal census for Burt Township listed 23 families residing at Indian Village, the 1910 census listed 29 families residing in the township.

Author Dale Van Every, born in northern Emmet County, Michigan, in 1894, wrote in his 1967 book, "Disinherited—The Lost Birthright of the American Indian, "The Indian, far more than the Negro, was a sore under the skin of the white man."

It is estimated that, when Christopher Columbus arrived in the New World, more than five million Indigenous people existed in North America. By the year 1900, that number was down to less than 300,000. Besides disease brought here from Europe, the United States government waged close to 1,500 attacks and raids on various Native Nations, tribes or bands. Federally funded or church-funded boarding schools tried to "kill the Indian" through forced assimilation. Some Cheboiganing Band children were away at the Holy Childhood boarding school in Harbor Springs and the Mount Pleasant boarding school when their homes were burned to the ground. Over 150 of these schools existed between the 1880s and the 1920s. From 1778 to 1871, the United States government entered into more than 500 treaties with the Native American tribes; all of these treaties have since been violated in some way or outright broken by the U.S. government.

Native American, Indigenous People, First Nation People, Indian or Anishinaabe People were not placed on the same level of hierarchy in American society as white Europeans. Treaties could be broken, children kidnapped and forced into boarding schools, lands seized over and over by illegal and immoral methods and means. After the December 1890 massacre at Wounded Knee, Chief Red Cloud, an Oglala-Lakota Sioux Ogima said "They made us many promises, but they kept only one. They promised to take our land — and they did."

Seven

Federal Government Intervention

On June 22, 1911, without any consultation with the Cheboiganing Band, the United States Department of Justice filed a 'Bill of Complaint" against John W. McGinn. Frank H. Watson, United States Attorney in the State of Michigan, filed the bill in the Eastern District of Michigan Federal Court's Northern Division in Bay City, Michigan. The court filing read:

"A Bill to Remove Cloud on the Title"

"The United States of America as guardian of the Cheboygan Band of Indians upon to-wit, the 23rd day of June, 1911 exhibited its original bill of complaint in this court against John W. McGinn, defendant therein, for the purpose of quieting title to certain lands of which the said Cheboygan Band of Indians are the owners in fee simple and which said lands the defendant claims some right, title or interest adverse to the title of said Cheboygan Band of Indians, and praying that the title of the said Cheboygan Band of Indians . . . might be decreed . . . and praying for other relief."

Watson concludes his Bill of Complaint by asking the court to ". . .

subpoena said John W. McGinn, thereby commanding him at a certain time under penalty of law to appear before this Honorable Court . . ."

Federal Prosecutor Watson makes it clear that the United States Justice Department acknowledged the existence of the Cheboiganing Band as an Indian Tribe (Band) under the protection of the United States!

A second federal government entity, the Department of the Interior, joined in the court case on the side of the Cheboiganing Band in January of 1912. Assistant Secretary Carmi A. Thompson wrote the Attorney General concerning the effort of the Cheboiganing Band to regain their lands. He stated, "The Department respectfully requests your consideration of the accompanying papers (1848-1850 in trust land patents), with a view to seeing if some action cannot be taken whereby these Indians may regain possession of their lands, lost through no apparent fault or negligence on their part."

Then, John W. McGinn died unexpectedly of a heart attack in his home in Cheboygan on Monday evening, January 8, 1912.

The lawsuit continued during the next two years during which there was great turnover in the Justice Department and in the federal court's Eastern District of Michigan. These turnovers did not help the Cheboiganing Band's court case. Each time someone new in Washington or in Michigan came into office, they had to be brought up to speed concerning the lawsuit. This was quite detrimental to the Band's chances of winning. The first turnover was Attorney General George Wickersham, who left office to be replaced by James McReynolds, then Ernest Knaebel, and then Thomas Watt Gregory.

In Michigan, the United States Attorney, Frank Watson, who initiated the case was replaced by Arthur Tuttle in August of 1911. Tuttle was then replaced by Clyde Webster after being picked to be the new Circuit Court Judge of the Eastern District of Michigan in June of 1913. In September of 1913, Judge Clarence Sessions, who had earlier taken over as the presiding judge in the case after the earlier resignation of Eastern District's Judge Alexis Angell (who had resigned in May of 1911) stated in court that it was his opinion the government needed to amend its case against the estate of John McGinn. The acting Attorney Ernest Knaebel wrote to Webster on February 16, 1914, stating "While the prospect of success does not seem brilliant, it strikes me as possible that we may be able to sustain the proposition that the lands held by these Indians appeals so strongly to the Justice Department that a question of law will be further investigated . . ."

The case of the United States vs. McGinn, et al., was amended by the federal government's Justice Department in May of 1914. The new "Bill of Complaint" now alleged that the facts tending to show that the assessment and levy of taxes under which the lands of the Cheboiganing Indians were sold by the State of Michigan were "irregular and invalid." The amended bill of complaint was seemingly prompted by the information provided the Attorney General by the Office of Indian Affairs. In late March of 1914, the Commissioner of Indian Affairs, Cato Sells, sent a special agent to Michigan to investigate the status of the Cheboiganing Indians.

Special Indian Agent Joseph W. Howell came to Brutus and took affidavits from Enos Cabinaw, Jane Grant and Albert Shananquet about what they witnessed and knew concerning the October 15, 1900 Burn-Out. Sells had received a letter in February of 1914 from Cabinaw stating the Cheboiganing Band believed there was an agreement between them and the United States government concerning no taxes on the "in trust lands" at Indian Village. Sells' response was to send Howell, who on April 14, 1914, issued a 17-page report after visiting various spots in the state of Michigan. Besides coming to Brutus, he also visited Detroit where he conferred with Clyde Webster who was handling the case at that time. Howell stopped in Grand Rapids before coming north.

During his interview in Brutus with Jane Grant, she told him that ". . . she was an eyewitness to the destruction of the village . . . and described the forcible removal of an old man who was carried out of his house on his bed and placed on the public highway. She also related that, while sick, Ms. Cabinaw was forcibly removed from her home. Mr. Cabinaw was also an eye-witness of the burning of the buildings."

Howell further reported that he had carefully inquired during these three interviews as to the origin of the money used by the Governor to purchase the Cheboiganing Band's land. He was told the money came from the funds the Government owed them from the 1836 Treaty of Washington, in other words, their negotiated annuity. The source of money had become part of the Justice Department's refiled "Bill of Complaint." Howell learned from the Brutus interviews the heart of the Cheboiganing Band's long-held belief that the 1836 Treaty's negotiated annuities were considered trust funds that could be converted into land for the benefit of the Band. Much like the interpretation of a treaty having to be what those who signed it (Anishinaabe) believed at the time, this was the case with the use of the annuity money. Howell further wrote in his report that he had formed a very favorable opinion of Cabinaw and the two others and their quest for justice. He also mentioned the Cheboiganing Band's high standing among the white population of the area and the large support from them for the Band regaining its ancestral land.

Howell traveled to Marquette to view the General Land Office records held there. The records confirmed the 1846-1850 purchases by the Governor and the land patent's wording concerning the "in trust to the Governor and his successors in office, forever." Then Howell proceeded to the county courthouse in Cheboygan to continue his fact-finding investigation.

Howell reported he learned from the tax history rolls that, from 1845 through 1860, no property tax had been levied on the 375 acres purchased by the Governor. From 1860 on, he found that "assessments were intermittently and irregularly made from time to time, and sometimes not at all." During various years in the beginning of the 1860s when the various tracts were assessed, the assessor failed to take into consideration the "in trust" nature of the property or the true owner (the Governor of Michigan and his successors in office, forever).

Joseph Howell's thorough investigation was the only one that actually examined the official records. It revealed the Cheboygan County treasurer's practice of advertising land parcels in the local newspaper for a short time whenever the tax titles were to be sold for delinquency. The ads were placed without reference to the owner's name, simply using the legal description of the property such as Lot 1, Township 36N, Range 3W, Section 28.

Howell wrote "It is undoubtedly true that the Indians had no personal knowledge of the proposed sale of their land. If the lands were taxable, the Indians were due constructive notice."

Howell also pointed out that when the writ of assistance and writ of possession were issued, the name of the property owner used was not the name of the Governor of the State who held the land in trust.

Howell traveled to Detroit in order to, once again, conference with the federal prosecutor in charge of the case, Clyde Webster. They both agreed that the "Bill of Complaint" should be amended and refiled. This new bill would center on the "irregularity of the proceedings" leading up to the sale of the 375 acres for back taxes. Howell revealed that he believed Judge Sessions was under the mistaken impression that the "in trust" lands purchased by the Governor as the trustee had, at some time, been translated into individual allotments as called for in the 1855 Treaty of Detroit. Howell also believed

Sessions was using some of the non-factual information contained in the 1903 Michigan Legislature Joint Resolution.

So, the final interview and conference during his trip took place in Grand Rapids with Judge Clarence Sessions. The Howell Report states, "I devoted about an hour and a quarter to a discussion of the case. . . He assured me that he was under no misapprehension as to the status of the lands in question, that he recognized the titles to such lands were obtained prior to the Treaty of 1855 . . ."

However, Sessions brought up the 1903 Resolution and how it suggested the "in trust" lands had been affected by the treaty. Of course, this was wrong. Copies of the Brutus affidavits were given to Sessions as well as copies of the data gleaned from the Marquette General Land Office.

Special Agent Howell then returned to his office in Washington, D.C., to finally check the archival records of the Office of Indian Affairs concerning their agent in Michigan, William Richmond, during the late 1840s. He put in his report that annuity money from the Treaty of 1836 was used by the Governor to purchase the Band's 375 ancestral acres.

"The lands were purchased for the Indians with funds due them as annuities, and that an arrangement was made with the consent of the Governor (Barry) of the State and the officers (William Richmond) of the United States to make the purchase in such a way as to redound (contribute) to their permanent benefit . . . this will indicate that the funds held in custody of the Government were invested in lands for the benefit of Agency Indians, and to effectuate (put into force) this benevolent plan, the Governor of the State accepted a conveyance in trust of the lands purchased with such funds, and that the trust was assumed as an official responsibility not only on his behalf, but also on the behalf of his successors in office."

Joseph Howell then closed his report with the following:

"I recommend that this report be furnished immediately to Mr. Ernest Knaebel, Assistant Attorney General, Department of Justice, together with its enclosures, and that a copy also be transmitted immediately to Mr. Clyde Webster, United States District Attorney, Detroit, Michigan."

Truly, Joseph W. Howell was a Good Samaritan.

In February of 1915, almost 15 years after the Burn-Out, United States District Attorney Clyde Webster wrote a letter to his boss, the Attorney General, and conveyed that he felt very encouraged about the Cheboiganing Band's chances in the new case. He stated that in a brief to Judge Sessions, he had brought out several arguments on behalf of the Band. He centered in on the true purpose and intent of the action to place the land in trust to the Governor and his successors. He noted the six patents had been issued between 1848 and 1850 during which time the Cheboiganing Indians were in an official tribal relationship with the federal government which began when the Band's Chief Chingassimo signed the Treaty of 1836. As time went on, the Band felt pressure to keep their Indian Village parcels intact. They knew they could not cope with the increasing number of white people coming into their area.

So, acting on advice from their local priest, their local state representative and their Indian Agent, Band members, determined to preserve their ancestral land, decided to each take some of their annuity money and have it sent to William Richmond, the Superintendent of the Mackinac Indian Agency in Detroit. It is quite evident that the Commissioner of Indian Affairs, who supervised William Richmond, and the President of the United States (if the matter was actually brought before him), sympathized with the purposes of the Cheboiganing Indians and their desire to keep their ancestral land. It must be assumed that the legal action taken by Richmond with the issuance of the patents "in trust" was created for the Band's protection under the guardianship of the United States over them and their property.

Webster's brief argued that these were active, not passive trusts. If the Band had simply wanted to buy land for their individual use, they would have done so. The Band and government officials decided to create an active trust to preserve the title for the Band by making it impossible for them to be alienated from the property.

In August of 1860, ten years after the last "in trust land" patent was issued, an attempt was made by a Band member to have the six deeds canceled and the 375 acres divided on an individual basis. Then-Michigan Governor Moses Misner was given a written request as the trustee of the land to do this and he refused.

Twelve years later, in 1872, Governor Henry Baldwin received another written request to have the "commonly held" lands divided and individually distributed. Once again a Michigan governor, as trustee of the land, refused to do so. Twice Michigan governors had been recognized as the land's trustee and been asked to subdivide the property, and twice they refused to do so. It was clear at this time the legality of a governor holding the Indian Village 375 acres "in trust" was recognized.

Judge Sessions   *Federal Court building, Bay City*

Eight

The Two Trials

The federal lawsuit involving the Cheboiganing Indians and the estate of John W. McGinn involved two trials in Bay City, Michigan. Federal District Attorney Clyde Webster was also a Good Samaritan for the Band, working hard and diligently on behalf of their interest. Webster was a University of Michigan law school graduate and, when appointed to the position of Federal District Attorney, was 35 years old. He took over the case in the summer of 1912 after his predecessor, Frank H. Watson, was not reappointed to his position by the new President Woodrow Wilson. Watson had been the one to initiate the Justice Department's case against McGinn in June of 1911. The Federal Circuit Court Judge for the Eastern District of Michigan, Alexis Angell, had just resigned and no one had been appointed as his replacement in June of 1911. That meant Grand Rapids Western District Federal Circuit Court Judge Clarence Sessions would preside over the case.

Once again, fate played a hand in the destiny of the Cheboiganing Band. It is quite possible that if Judge Alexis Angell had been on the bench during the case, a different outcome may have been achieved. Judge Angell was the son of James Angell, who served as the President of the University of Michigan for almost 30 years until resigning in 1909. James Angell was a noted abolitionist and liberal thinker and that may have also filtered down to his son. Judge Clarence Sessions also graduated from the University of Michigan, however, he did not attend its law school nor any other. His background in law came from his "reading law" and working under an attorney as an apprentice. He was a Michigan Circuit Court Judge prior to being appointed to the federal bench in March of 1911, three months prior to the Justice Department filing its "Bill of Complaint" against John McGinn.

Thus, the second federal court case against McGinn began with the filing of briefs in February of 1915. A court "brief" is simply an attorney's view of the facts of the case in his own words. It should clearly state the issues and argue them in order to persuade the court in favor of one's client. Webster's brief concluded:

1. These lands were purchased from the federal government using the 1836 Treaty annuity money. The title for each parcel was specifically written to place it "in trust to the Governor of Michigan and his successors in office, forever."

2. The trust had been created by authorities of the United States so that no state law or state action could interfere with it.

3. From the beginning, the Cheboiganing Band lacked legal ability to convey (sell or give) away their "in trust" property unless authorized by the federal government.

4. This above rule applied to the Band, regardless whether or not they had been citizens of the United States.

5. The guardianship of the United States government is terminated only by its own clear and unequivocal act.

6. Indian lands inalienable by them cannot be taken from them by state taxation. The assessment, levy, and sale of these lands, and the tax deeds based thereon, were and are totally invalid.

The egregious misinterpretation in the case involved Article Five in the 1855 Treaty of Detroit. The Article was requested by the various Anishinaabe bands of Michigan as a way to correct certain wording used in the 1836 Treaty of Washington. In the first treaty, the Ottawa "Nation" and Chippewa "Nation" wording was used and it irritated the leaders of the Michigan bands. No tribe or nation ever existed in the area known as Michigan. Each band was on its own and, from time to time, a confederacy of such bands would be set up to deal with various issues. Article Five's wording was confusing when created to fix the "Nation" problem. It stated:

"The tribal organization of said Ottawa and Chippewa Indians, except so far as may be necessary for the purpose of carrying into effect the provisions of this agreement, is hereby dissolved; and if at any time hereafter, further negotiations with the United States in reference to any matters contained herein, should become necessary, no general convention of the Indians shall be called; but such as reside in the vicinity of any usual place of payment, or those only who are immediately interested in the questions involved, may arrange all matters between themselves and the United States, without the concurrence of other portions of their people, and as fully and conclusively, and with the same effect in every respect, as if all were represented."

The wording was confusing in 1855 and in 1900, 1903 and 1915 and later.

Article Five wording did not mean the Anishinaabe bands of Michigan were no longer the political organizations of these bands. The true meaning was supposed to clarify that actual political jurisdiction was returned to the individual bands, where it had been all along. Bands would always be the Michigan political units that would work with the federal government. However, that was not what later interpretations would profess and it was very harmful to the Cheboiganing Band.

Also, during the negotiations for the 1855 Treaty of Detroit, the journal minutes kept by government clerks had their notes in the margins, which actually helped explain the true meaning of Article Five. Those margin notes also explained what the Anishinaabe negotiators and their translators believed when it came to paying taxes. Dr. Richard White found various band leaders had asked for the guarantee that any lands granted in the treaty and those that were previously purchased would be exempt from taxes. Office of Indian Affairs George Manypenny, who negotiated the treaty, was found to have told the leaders that "on the question of taxes he was disposed to manage that for your benefit."

The Band leaders took that as meaning tax exemption. In the case of the Cheboiganing Band, that was true for a few years after the treaty was ratified. No taxes were levied, as should have been the case.

Article Five simply meant that the federal government would now recognize the individual bands in Michigan rather than the Ottawa Nation or the Chippewa Nation. It dissolved the idea of two nations governing the Michigan Anishinaabe so that each band would be correctly dealing in the future with the federal government after 1855. However, because it was so poorly written, many federal officials down the road would misinterpret it as meaning the Michigan Anishinabee no longer had any political organizations or units. Every time there was a new administrator in the Department of Interior or in its Office of Indian Affairs, it was a new opinion rather than checking the 1855 Treaty journal and its notes to find out the facts. It became a nightmare for the Cheboiganing Band by the 1890s.

Secretary of the Interior Columbus Delano was one of the first federal officials to misinterpret Article Five. He did so in 1872 when he misspoke, offering his false opinion that "Michigan Indians no longer had any tribal ties" to the Office of Indian Affairs, over which he was the head administrator. That false opinion began to filter down to the Mackinac Indian Agency personnel in Michigan. In his December 1900 message to the Michigan Legislature, Governor Pingree once again mistakenly mentioned the 1855 Treaty's dissolution of Michigan's Anishinaabe Bands' political organizations. He also mistakenly said that it was under the 1855 Treaty provisions for allotments that the Cheboiganing Band had purchased their 375 acres, thus making them taxable. Wrong opinion after wrong opinion by federal and state officials became policy and permanently wronged the Cheboiganing Band.

The most damaging use of the Article Five language misinterpretation was when Michigan House of Representative's Charles Pierce used some of it he had found in Governor Pingree's message written in the June 1903 Joint Resolution. That piece of legislation was finally a real attempt to give aid and comfort to the Cheboiganing Band. Unfortunately, it did the opposite! Pierce wrote the following concerning Article Five:

"Whereas, the unfortunate situation in which these Indians were placed was called to the attention of the federal government and received in reply the dictum of the Secretary of the Interior that 'It is not within the powers of this department to afford any relief' was received."

The Secretary of Interior at that time in 1900 was Ethan Hitchcock.

He, once again, without checking the records, offered the egregious misinterpretation of the 1855 Treaty's Article Five. It would not be the last time it would happen, causing great harm to the Cheboiganing Band.

After being appointed to the McGinn case in January of 1912, District Attorney Tuttle knew he was not prepared to argue the case on behalf of the Band due to not being familiar with the facts of the case.

In fact, he asked Judge Sessions for a continuance and it was granted. It should be noted that the case in Bay City's federal courtroom was originally slated to be argued by William H. Lewis. He was the first Black American appointed as a Federal District Attorney in Massachusetts by President Theodore Roosevelt in 1903.

Then, in 1910, he was one of the first Black Americans appointed to be one of the five Assistant Attorney Generals in Washington, D.C. That appointment was made by President William H. Taft. In 1911, Lewis was also one of the first Black Americans to be admitted to the American Bar Association. It was Lewis and Willis N. Mills, a special assistant to Lewis, who wrote the June 1911 15-page "Writ of Subpoena" for the Justice Department against McGinn. In 1912, Lewis was to have come to Bay City as a special federal prosecutor to plead the government's case. However, he became quite ill and could not make the journey. Lewis would go on to be a noted advocate for Civil Rights in the United States.

Thus, the McGinn case dragged on with the Bill of Complaint in the Equity Court. Eventually, Clyde Webster took charge of matters and deeply studied the government's case against McGinn. One of his first actions was to ask Washington for a copy of Lewis' brief. That brief was never forthcoming and Lewis, by then, was a private attorney back in Boston. What Webster did receive in the form of help was the appointment of the former Michigan Assistant Attorney General for the State of Michigan as a Special Assistant to Webster. Arthur Hicks was very familiar with the facts of the case and was eager to help the federal government. Hicks was now a private attorney in Detroit and had given the case his personal attention since it began in 1911. He was paid $50 for his time.

Webster did not obtain the "brief" prepared by Lewis. Lewis was not reappointed by the new president, Woodrow Wilson, and left office in January, 1913. In September of 1913, Webster wrote to new Attorney General James McReynolds stating the McGinn case, which had begun in June of 1911, might be transferred from the federal court of equity to the law side of the federal court (the Court of Law) in which Judge Sessions would still preside. The possible change was due to the Supreme Court's adopting New Equity Rules in November of 1912. Equity Court cases were those involving real estate. The word "equity" means what is fair. Judge Sessions had suggested to both parties that the case, begun as an Equity Court case, might be best refiled as a Court of Law case. One of the Supreme Court's new rules was Rule No. 22, which allowed for such a transfer. It read:

"If at any time it appears that a suit commenced in equity should have been brought as an action on the law side of the court, it shall be forthwith transferred to the law side and be there proceeded with, with only such alteration in the pleadings as shall be essential."

Meanwhile, Webster went on to write McReynolds that he was now wondering if Article Five of the 1855 Treaty had meant that Michigan bands had been dissolved and no longer had formal relations with the United States government. He was worried that meant the Cheboiganing Band was no longer under the guardianship of the Office of Indian Affairs nor the Justice Department. He was afraid he had no jurisdiction to try the case in either the Court of Equity or the Court of Law. Thus, he was asking the new Attorney General for his thoughts on the matter. Once again, Article Five surfaced in the mind of a federal official. Also, Webster wondered in his letter whether the Band members had actually become United States citizens as a result of the 1887 Dawes Act passed by Congress. If so, did citizenship create a problem for his case in either court?

In a follow-up letter dated September 13, 1913, Webster told McReynolds that he had secured the assistance of Arthur Hicks and had been furiously trying to thoroughly familiarize himself with the facts of the case. He stated he was waiting for McReynolds to reply to his earlier letter due to Hicks being concerned whether the band members' 375 acres "in trust" had actually been part of the allotted lands from the government noted in the 1855 Treaty. Webster asked that the Office of Indian Affairs records be searched for answers.

A partial answer to Webster's and Hick's questions came from Washington on September 16, 1913. One of McReynolds' Assistant Attorney Generals, Ernest Knaeble, wrote back stating, "I have to advise you that the Interior Department reports that Townships 35 and 36N,

Range 3W were set apart for these Indians under the Treaty of July 31, 1855. However, it seems immaterial whether or not these Indians received allotments. It has been distinctly held that the political status of these Indians does not condition the power of the government to protect their property."

The Assistant Attorney (unnamed) went on to advise the two district attorneys in Michigan that: ". . . if they did receive citizenship, that status did not deprive the United States of its power nor relieve it of its duty to control their property or protect their rights."

Clearly, the Justice Department was 100% behind the new lawsuit in Judge Sessions' federal court of law.

Webster, by the end of September 1913, told his superiors in the Department of Justice by letter, "I have great hopes of winning on the law side of the Court. These cases cited in our brief seem to be exceptionally good. If you have further suggestions to offer, I would be glad indeed to receive them."

The case dragged on through the rest of 1913 into 1914, however, it remained in Judge Sessions' Federal Court of Equity. On January 16, 1914, in what was to be the first John McGinn case, Sessions rendered his opinion in Equity Court. Clyde Webster sent a letter dated that day to Acting Attorney Ernest Knaeble, who was now in charge of the Justice Department due to the resignation of McReynolds. Knaeble had been in the Attorney General's office since 1907, first working as a Special Assistant to Attorney General George Wickersham. He had been put in charge of the Justice Department's Public Lands Division in 1911, as an Assistant Attorney General, and argued many public lands and Indian land cases on their behalf.

Webster told Knaeble that Sessions had sustained the "demurrer" in the case argued by Watts Humphrey, one of the McGinn family attorneys in the case; the same Watts Humphrey who was known as a "tax shark" in Cheboygan County and for whom Dr. Richard White in his research had found was the first to obtain a "tax title" for land at Indian Village in 1873. By the time of the trial, Humphrey and George Grant had formed a law firm in Saginaw, Michigan, specializing in both law and equity cases in federal or state courts. His firm also represented many large railroads and companies in Michigan. A "demurrer" meant that Humphrey had argued against the government's Bill of Complaint on the grounds that it should be dismissed because it failed to state sufficient facts to constitute a cause of action. That action would have been for McGinn's estate to vacate the 375 acres of "in trust land."

Judge Sessions decided to grant the "demurrer" to the McGinn family attorneys on the grounds that, in his mind, the six "in trust" land patents, written in part by William Richmond with the knowledge of Governor John Barry, did not use explicit enough wording concerning no alienation from land due to taxes. Richmond had not spelled it out firmly enough for Sessions. It seemed Judge Sessions did not believe a legal federal government document had to be interpreted the same way a federal treaty with an Indian tribe or band had to be interpreted. The Supreme Court 1899 ruling in the Jones vs. Meehan case had ruled:

"A treaty between the United States and an Indian tribe must be construed not according to the technical meaning of its words to learned lawyers, but in the sense in which they would naturally be understood by the Indians."

Thus, in Sessions' mind, a legal document such as a General Land Office land patent did not fall under the same category. Everything in it, according to Sessions, had to be explicitly written out, even though the only possible meaning of using the words "in trust to the Governor of Michigan and his successors in office forever" was no alienation for any reason!

Sessions also wrote in his January 6 decision on granting the "demurrer" that, in doing so, he had referred to the 1903 Michigan Legislature Joint Resolution wording concerning the 1855 Treaty, which he stated, he believed said these lands ". . . were reserved for the Cheboygan Indians for a definite period of time and then patented directly to the Indians according to their several selections, after which time the lands were held by the Indians as real estate is held by other citizens of the State and were taxed the same as other lands."

Why did Sessions bring up the 1903 Joint Resolution? It had not been referred to in court by the Justice Department attorneys working to help the Band. That resolution would surface again after the judge allowed the case to be continued by amending the original Bill of Complaint.

In early 1914, the Department of Justice had to decide whether to appeal the case against McGinn or drop it. Band member and acting leader Enos Cabinaw wrote letters to both the Interior Department and Justice

Department asking for them to resume the case. What Acting Attorney General Ernest Knaeble was pondering was whether to refile the Bill of Complaint in the Federal District's Court of Law, or refile in the same Court of Equity.

Either way, Judge Clarence Sessions would continue to preside over the case. On March 5, 1914, Watts Humphrey wrote to Clyde Webster a letter in which he asked why the Justice Department might amend their first Bill of Complaint. He suggested that Webster and the Attorney General's office in Washington did not understand the facts in the case as he did. One of Humphrey's facts was his belief that the 375 "in trust" acres were somehow connected to the parcels of land allotted to some Band members under the provisions of the 1855 Treaty of Detroit.

Humphrey also somehow contended that the Cheboiganing Band members were full citizens of the State of Michigan and some of them had even voted in presidential elections. He based this on the wording of the 1850 Michigan Constitution, which was open to interpretation. Most people at the time believed the granting of citizenship was only to Metis (mixed European-Indian ancestry) and only to those who had given up their "tribal affiliation." Clearly, the Cheboiganing Band members were not all Metis, nor did they give up their membership with the Band.

The federal government, at this time, certainly did not regard Anishinaabe people of Michigan as citizens of the United States. During the Civil War, the Office of Indian Affairs ruled that Indian Bands who signed the 1855 Treaty of Detroit were not citizens and could not be drafted. In 1871, the federal government ruled that Indians could not take or receive lands under the 1862 Homestead Act.

So, in practice, the Cheboiganing Band members were not considered full citizens with equal rights and responsibilities as other white citizens. They occupied a "special status." It was not until 1924 that Congress passed the Indian Citizenship Act, which granted universal citizenship to any Native American born in the United States. Congress was prompted to pass this legislation to help honor the number of Native Americans who enlisted in the military during World War I.

Making a decision to proceed by Knaeble came in early May of 1914. He wrote Secretary of Interior Franklin Lane, the third time since the June 1911 beginning of the lawsuit, and stated in this May 5 letter ". . . I have the honor to advise you . . . the government's bill has been amended so as to allege facts tending to show that the assessment and the levy of taxes under which the lands of the Cheboygan Indians were sold by the state, were irregular and invalid."

The decision was prompted by Joseph Howell's April 1914 report. Knaebel stated as such ". . . these amendments were largely based upon the recent investigation by Mr. Howell of your department. It is hoped the lands involved may ultimately be recovered for the Indians."

Acting Attorney General Knaebel's decision made him one more "Grand Good Samaritan." He correctly believed in what the Howell Report of April 1914 had stated. The tax assessments, begun in 1860 on the 375 acres of "in trust land," were done without considering the trust nature of those lands nor the true owner of the title, the Governor of Michigan. Knaebel found that assessments were made intermittently and irregularly from time to time, and sometimes not at all. Howell also wrote in his report that when the six parcels of land were purchased with government annuity money and the land patents written in a certain way, it was to ensure permanent benefit to the Cheboiganing Band and had the consent of the then-Governor of Michigan. He did this as an official responsibility of his office and for his successors in office.

The second trial was set to begin on May 5, 1914, three years after the first trial began and two years after John McGinn's death. In the new Bill of Complaint, written by Clyde Webster and filed in the Federal Court of Equity, Bay City, on April 30, 1914, the following was stated:

> 1. "The monies with which these lands were purchased were monies payable to the Cheboygan Band of Indians as annuities, and by agreement with the Band and the Superintendent of the Mackinac Indian Agency, were turned over to the Governor of Michigan. The purpose thereof was to create an active trust with the view to prevent the sale of the lands by the Indians themselves, or for debts or for taxes. Indian trust funds (annuities) were converted into land for the benefit of the entire Band.

> 2. "These lands were thus conveyed by the United States between the years 1845-1850 to the Governor of Michigan as trustee for the Cheboygan Indians. These lands were not taxed for 15 years until 1860. Beginning in that year, assessments were made intermittently and irregularly from

time to time.

3. "At the proceedings resulting in the writs of assistance, the Band was not represented by any authorized attorney they had secured. They had no notice of those proceedings."

The fact that the legal title to these lands was in the name of the Governor of Michigan in trust for the Cheboiganing Indians was not taken into consideration in these proceedings. The Band knew nothing about their land being taxed or about any tax sales. They were never given notice of the writs, about being taxed, nor the tax sales.

District Attorney Webster also elaborated in his new Bill of Complaint on how County Treasurer William Maultby had refused to assess or collect taxes on this land. Or how, after he left office, the Band never received any written notice of a tax assessment, nor did the then-Governor of the State. He also pointed out that, when newspaper publication of the tax sales took place, the owners of the described lands were given as "unknown" when, in fact, public records showed them to be owned "in trust by the Governor of Michigan."

The new Bill of Complaint listed the United States of America as Guardian of the Cheboiganing Indians, the Complainant. Frank Shepard and Albert Ramsey were named as executors of the John McGinn estate and were the Defendants. The estate's attorney Watts Humphrey, now of Saginaw, argued that the 1855 Treaty of Detroit's Article Five had dissolved the political status of the Cheboiganing Band and thus the federal government could not act as their guardian in the case, the same egregious misinterpretation that had appeared many times before to the detriment of the Band.

Grant and Humphrey also argued that since no Band member's names had appeared in the new Bill of Complaint, none must still have been living by May of 1914. That seemed to be a fallacious argument at best. They also noted, in their answer to the lawsuit, that the wording in the six land patents did not say, in specific-enough words, that the lands were inalienable due to taxes, that they were not meant to be an active trust. They also tried to argue that the statute of limitations prohibited the filing of the lawsuit in 1911 since it was ten years after McGinn's possession had taken place.

Judge Sessions postponed the case until October of 1914 and it dragged on into February of 1915. At that time, Judge Sessions ruled on Humphrey's "motion to dismiss" the case. He denied that motion and in doing so said, ". . . The case comes down to whether these lands belonged to the Indians as a Tribe, or were held in trust for them as a Tribe. If so, they could not be conveyed or alienated and, hence, were not subject to taxation."

Sessions ended his decision to not dismiss with some troubling words that portrayed the future. He wrote, "In view of the Treaty of 1855 with the Ottawa and Chippewa Indians, by the express terms of which tribal organizations were dissolved . . . and holding that the absence of primary restrictions as to any alienation."

He was showing that he was under the spell of the Article Five fallacy and that the wording used by Superintendent William Richmond beginning in 1845, "in trust to the Governor of Michigan and his successors in office, forever," was not specific enough for him.

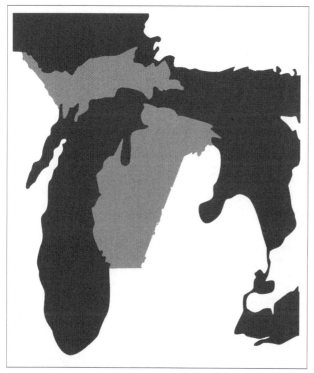

The Treaty of 1836 ceded the light gray area shown here in the eastern Upper Peninsula and the northwestern Lower Peninsula of Michigan.

Albert Shananquet   *Albert Shananquet*

Nine

The Verdict and its Aftermath

The presiding judge in the case, Clarence William Sessions, was born in a small farming town in Ionia County, Michigan, in 1859. His father, William, was a farmer. By age 21, he was a lawyer in the town of Ionia, Michigan. According to the 1905 *Michigan Alumnus* magazine, he attended the University of Michigan from 1889-1891, leaving at the end of his junior year to study law. He then "read law" at the law firm of Mitchell, Bell and McGarry in Ionia before leaving and going into the lumber business in western Michigan. He later resumed reading law at the Ionia law firm and, in the spring of 1884, was admitted to the Ionia County Bar Association.

Reading law was somewhat common at the time. Abraham Lincoln had done the same before becoming a lawyer. Sessions had married at age 23, and, by 1885, was in law practice in Muskegon, Michigan. He was city attorney for five years and, in 1902, joined the law firm of Nims, Hoyt, Erwin, Sessions, and Vanderwerp. The firm represented large banks and lumber interests in western Michigan. In November

1905, Sessions ran on the Republican ticket for Circuit Court Judge and won. He took office in January of 1906, presiding over part of Oceana and Muskegon counties.

In 1911, Republican President William Howard Taft nominated Sessions to the federal bench for the Western District of Michigan. One of his first cases to preside over came to him as a fluke. Arthur Tuttle, who had been in the federal District Attorney's office for the Eastern District of Michigan, had to recuse himself from the Cheboiganing Band case.

Tuttle's background was opposite of Sessions' conservative Republican Party ideology, therefore it is likely the verdict concerning the Bill of Complaint would have been different had Tuttle been able to sit on the bench for the case. Judge Sessions was given the case even though his courtroom was in Grand Rapids, and he had to make time to travel to Bay City, Michigan, where the case in the Northern Division of the Eastern District was to be heard.

The federal government's case against the McGinn estate to "Remove the Cloud on the Title" carried through 1915 and into 1916. The McGinn estate attorneys continued to falsely tell Judge Sessions that the Band knew about paying their property taxes, and the Band had also been represented by an attorney (Ben Halstead who they had no knowledge of at the time) in the 1898 writs of assistance proceedings. These same attorneys also continued to claim that, in the 1898 writ proceedings, the Governor of Michigan was made aware of what was taking place, though they could offer no proof. They also put forth a statute of limitations argument, as well as to argue the Article Five fallacy.

The McGinn attorneys even included the false idea that the Band members were citizens, and since they were no longer a band (political organization), it meant that the Justice Department had no standing to act in the case as their Guardian. They further falsely argued that in 1845, the Governor of Michigan, John Barry, was not acting in his official capacity when he agreed to the wording of the Cheboiganing Indians' patent.

Then, these attorneys made a false claim to the judge that Cheboiganing Band members had occupied the 400 acres offered them under the 1903 Joint Resolution, thus the resolution's "moral obligation by the state" had been met. Of course, that was not true. Their final argument concerned their allegation that McGinn made permanent and valuable improvements to the 375 acres on Indian Point, increasing the value to over $40,000 ($1.2 million in 2023 dollars) and, as such, the land should not be vacated.

Besides obfuscating the facts of the case, it would appear that the McGinn attorney team had a strategy of stalling and dragging out the case. In January of 1916, Webster wrote to his superior in Washington, D.C., Attorney General Thomas Watt Gregory, the third one involved in the case. He requested that the Justice Department ask the Interior Department to send Special Agent Joseph Howell to Michigan to assist in the case. In February of 1916, Attorney General Gregory sent Clyde Webster a possible "smoking gun" of evidence to support the Band's claims regarding their ancestral land. Joseph Howell had unearthed certain files in the Office of Indian Affairs archives.

The evidence found in the archives was a series of correspondence between the Michigan Mackinac Indian Agency and Washington. It was then sent by the Interior Department's Assistant Secretary Bo Sweeney to the Attorney General Gregory for use in the case. Along with the possible "smoking gun" evidence, Sweeney also pointed out in his letter to Gregory, that the Cheboiganing Band of Indians were, at that time, under the guardianship of the United States via the supervision of the United States Indian Agency at Bay Mills, Michigan.

The evidence was grouped into five classifications:

Group I: "Showing administration and supervision generally of the Affairs of the Chippewa and Ottawa Tribes (of which the Cheboiganing Band was a part), parties to the treaties of 1836 and 1855."

Group II: "Showing various purchases of lands in bodies for the Chippewa and Ottawa Indians with annuity moneys at different times and places, and the supervision of Government officers, as well as the cooperation of the Governor of the State of Michigan, relating to such purchases."

Group III: "Showing supervision by officers of the United States over the schools of the Chippewa and Ottawa Indians, and assistance extended by the Government of the United States to such schools by furnishing books and other school supplies."

Group IV: "Showing supervision by officers of the United States over the Chippewa and Ottawa Indians in connection with farming and milling operations, and the expenditure by the Government of funds on behalf of the Indians for agricultural improvements, livestock, et cetera."

Group V: "Showing the supervision of officers of the Government of the United States with respect to the reservation of lands for the Chippewa and Ottawa Indians pursuant to provisions of the Treaty of 1855."

Group I evidence was a series of letters of correspondence with Washington from Michilimackinac Indian Agency personnel beginning in 1836. Letters from Henry Schoolcraft and William Richmond were in this group. Also, a 1858 letter from the then Commissioner of Indian Affairs to the Mackinac Indian Agency in Detroit giving instructions and jurisdiction over all Indians in Michigan. This clearly refuted the false idea that became the misinterpretation that Article Five of the 1855 Treaty dissolved all Michigan Bands, and thus federal government guardianship. Another letter from Washington in 1870 confirmed such federal supervision and guardianship.

Group II contained evidence through letters of correspondence that the practice of using the 1836 Treaty annuity money to buy land for the benefit of Michigan Indians began in 1839, and the government annuity trust funds were being converted into real estate. The November 25, 1844, letter from Robert Stuart, the Mackinac Agency Superintendent on Mackinac Island, was very telling. It stated, "I am glad the Indians have purchased lands, and will, in the course of the winter, try to think of some way in which to secure them, else they will, I fear, be taken for debts, et cetera."

Stuart then writes to Father Xavier Pierz, the local Catholic priest in the area of northern Michigan, in November of 1844. He states to Pierz, "You and I must next summer consult and try to get their lands secured in some other ways."

Dr. Richard White felt strongly that Pierz and Stuart most certainly decided that the only way to secure the land in posterity for the Indians was to deed such lands to the Governor of Michigan. White also concluded in his 1978 research on the subject that:

"The decision to put the land in trust to the Governor of Michigan, rather than the President of the United States simply followed the logic of the events at that time in the country. In the South, states had successfully extended their laws and jurisdiction over Indian peoples and, in Michigan, the Governor was now asserting the same right. If government protection was to be secured, it was logical that the Governor of Michigan was to be the future guardian of the Indians within the State's boundaries . . . Stuart and Pierz in 1845 were merely anticipating a development which they thought inevitable . . . Governor Barry had to have been involved. William Richmond, Robert Stuart's successor as Superintendent, then acted as the intermediary in the purchase of land for the Band . . . The purchase seemed to represent a transfer of land still under federal trusteeship to the trusteeship of the Governor of Michigan. The land purchased was within the 1,000-acre reserve secured under the Treaty of 1836 and contained the site of the Band's village."

Group III evidence shows, through letters of correspondence, the connection of the Cheboiganing Band to the Office of Indian Affairs during the 1850s, 1860s and 1870s via the schoolhouse and teacher the federal government provided the Band. The first schoolhouse and teacher began in January of 1858. This period was long after the Treaty of 1855 and its Article Five. Group IV deals with the United States Indian Agency supplying agricultural supplies. Group V deals with the formation of reservations in Michigan negotiated in the Treaty of 1855.

In April of 1916, Webster began to show his frustration with Judge Sessions and the judge's failure to put the hearing of the five-year-old case on his docket. He wrote to Assistant Attorney General Ernest Knaebel on April 8.

"I received a letter from Mr. Howell of the Office of Indian Affairs of the Department of Interior inquiring about the case. I will enclose what I said back to him. I am as discouraged as ever about getting the case on the docket for a hearing. I have tried my best to get Judge Sessions to give us a day. He promised he would in February but another case took up our time. Now Watts Humphrey has died and no one in his office knows anything about the case."

Webster's successor in office in Detroit, John Kinnane, then asked permission to go to Grand Rapids to see Judge Sessions about a hearing. It was granted, however, he did not make the trip, so the case continued into 1917. Kinnane took over from Clyde Webster in August of 1917. He would be the fourth Federal District Attorney involved in the case.

He asked for the presence of Special Agent Joseph Howell to assist him. We know that Howell's report in April of 1914 was very specific and helpful to the Cheboiganing Indians. He was one who possessed the true facts of the case. He knew why and how the patent wording was such, and why it meant no alienation for any reason. Howell had held several conferences with Kinnane's predecessor, Clyde Webster. Finally, Sessions set aside Wednesday, May 16, 1917, for the hearing in Bay City.

The last hearing in the six-year-long case of the United States vs. John McGinn finally took place. A federal case to "Remove the Cloud on Title" officially titled "The United States of America as Guardian of the Cheboygan Band of Indians, Complainant, vs. John McGinn, et al., Defendant."

Kinnane made his final appeal for the return of the Cheboiganing Indian lands that he argued had been unjustly alienated from the group. He was aided in the courtroom by Special Agent Joseph Howell. By that time, both John McGinn and his attorney friend Watts Humphrey had passed away. It is not known who appeared opposite District Attorney Kinnane to give the final arguments for the McGinn side of the case.

Howell had left for Michigan by train from Washington, D.C., on May 8, 1917. He was sent by Cato Sells, the Commissioner of Indian Affairs, who headed the Office of Indian Affairs. On May 19, District Attorney Kinnane wrote to Attorney General Gregory a letter detailing the hearing. "I have the honor to report that the case of the United States vs. John McGinn was tried out before Judge Sessions sitting at Bay City. The case has finally been completed so far as the evidence and the arguments are concerned . . . We have the assurance of the Court that the case will be speedily decided . . . The government case developed very satisfactorily and the showing is such that we are hopeful for a favorable decision. The case on behalf of the government was handled by Joseph W. Howell of the Office of Indian Affairs. He both actively participated in the preparation and trial . . . We feel that everything possible has been done to present with all its force the contention and position of the government and the Indians."

Kinnane later wrote that Howell's work was excellent and that he should be given high commendation. The Attorney General's office sent a letter to the Interior Department stating such about Howell.

Correspondence from Joseph Howell to John Kinnane showed that he was very optimistic that the facts he presented would help win the case for the Band. The cooperation between the Office of Indian Affairs and the Justice Department had been very positive. Judge Sessions listened for three days to the oral arguments. It then took only 12 days for the optimism to fade. On Thursday, May 31,1917, Sessions issued his verdict.

In the District Court of the United States for the Eastern District of Michigan, the Northern Division," Sessions wrote, "If the plaintiff can prevail, it must be upon the theory that the Government, either by the peculiar and specific terms of the original conveyances to the Cheboiganing Band of Indians, or by virtue of some general right of guardianship over these Indians and their property, has reserved and, at all times, retained such control and dominion over these lands as to make them inalienable without its consent, and therefore, nontaxable."

After six long years, Judge Clarence Sessions took only 12 days to rule against the United States Department of Justice and the Cheboiganing Band of Ottawa and Chippewa Indians. A large part of the Sessions' ruling was centered around the 1855 Treaty of Detroit's Article Five's false belief that it had dissolved any and all tribal organization of the Michigan Ottawa and Chippewa Bands. Article Five wording did not mean the Anishinaabe bands of Michigan were no longer the political organizations of these bands. The true meaning was supposed to clarify that actual political jurisdiction was returned to the individual bands where it had been all along. It got rid of the word Nations that had been used in the 1836 Treaty of Washington. Bands, not Nations or Tribes, had always been the true Michigan Anishinaabe political units.

Judge Sessions had been told as such by Office of Indian Affairs Special Agent Joseph Howell in April of 1917. Without a doubt, he was told that a second time by Howell during the May 1917 final hearing. However, Sessions ignored the facts! He also relied in his ruling on the wrong information contained in the 1903 Joint Resolution written by Michigan Clerk of the House of Representatives Charles Pierce. One of the pieces of wrong information Pierce used was the quoted statement from the Secretary of Interior in 1900, Ethan Hitchcock, "It is not within the powers of this department to afford any relief to the Cheboiganing

Band."

It was wrong when first given and wrong to use in the verdict, even though the evidence presented to Sessions by the government showed that the Article Five fallacy was irrelevant. And, the specific wording of the six Cheboiganing land patents was done to secure no alienation for any reason from their land parcels. Sessions ignored those facts. Sessions wrote in his verdict he found no limitation or restriction in the words "in trust to the Governor of Michigan and his successors in office, forever."

What did he think that meant when he further claimed the six patents conveyed "perfect title to the lands without any restriction upon the power of alienation?"

He also wrote that the money used to buy the 375 acres came from an individual Indian's purse, ignoring the evidence that it was government trust money from their annuities used to create an "active trust" against land alienation.

Finally, Sessions falsely wrote in his verdict that "the Cheboygan Indians were a small Band and have never been treated, considered, recognized as a nation or tribe."

What? Beginning on March 31, 1836, when Chief Chingassimo signed his X to the treaty, one he helped negotiate in Washington, D.C., the Cheboiganing Band was a federally recognized Indian political unit in Michigan. Sessions was wrong on every count he used to dismiss the Bill of Complaint. In many minds, A Cloud Was Now Really Over the Land.

It is apparent that the Sessions ruling came from the Watts Humphrey playbook that he laid out as a defense for John McGinn seizing the land and burning the log houses at Indian Village. After his death, every false argument Humphrey came up with was used by his law firm to perpetuate the false legality of the land alienation and burning.

It did not matter that the Office of Indian Affairs Special Agent could refute the false arguments with actual facts. Sessions ignored them.

Ten

Generations of Patience

In summary, the Northwest Ordinance of 1787, officially titled "An Ordinance for the Government of the Territory of the United States Northwest of the Ohio River," contained a specific reference to the Indigenous People of that area. Article Three stated:

"The utmost good faith shall always be observed towards the Indians; their land and property shall never be taken from them without their consent; and in their property, rights, and liberty, they shall never be invaded or disturbed unless in just and lawful wars authorized by Congress. Laws founded in justice and humanity shall from time to time be made for preventing wrongs being done to them, and for preserving peace and friendship with them."

The United States Supreme Court's "Canons of Construction" are the foundational principles of federal Indian law. They require No. 1 "that all treaties be interpreted as the Indians would have understood them

---

The Native American patience symbol consists of a large, unfilled circle that contains a V shape, where the meeting of two diagonal lines is at the base point of the circles, and the end of each line extends beyond the circular boundary. The symbol represents patience and perseverance.

at the time of signing. And, No. 2 that "all treaties are to be liberally construed in favor of the Indians with all the ambiguities resolved in their favor. These cannons have been in place since 1832 and were written by Supreme Court Justice John McLean in the famous Georgia vs. Worchester case. This case established the precedent that the United States federal government had constitutional authority that overrode any state law. The ruling affirmed that the federal government had the exclusive power to enter into treaties with other nations, whether foreign or domestic, such as Michigan's Anishinaabe Bands.

The Cheboiganing Band signed, in good faith, the 1836 Treaty of Washington. It involved their ancestral land at Indian Point, part of the overall 13.7 million acres of ancestral land belonging to Anishinaabe Bands in Michigan. Those 13.7 million acres were to be ceded to the federal government. In return, some of the negotiated items for the Bands were 20 years of annual payments (annuities), medical services in perpetuity, and hunting, fishing and gathering rights in perpetuity. Also, for the Cheboiganing Band, a 1000-acre reservation at Indian Point, where their Indian Village was located, was to be created.

It did not take but a few months for the Band to recognize that the "white man" spoke with a "forked tongue." When the treaty was brought back to Michigan, some of the earlier negotiated language had been changed. A few United States Senators rewrote part of the treaty before agreeing to vote to ratify it. Now, instead of a 1000-acre reservation in perpetuity, the new language said for only five years unless further extended by Congress. This change was hard for the Band to understand and, in fact, caused Chief Chingassimo to eventually gather others and leave for Canada's Manitoulin Island.

To make sure that Indian Village would remain in their hands, Band members, now at this point, turned to another possible way to ensure its land protection. It was a formal legal document known as a United States General Land Office land patent. Following the advice of their priest, their Michigan State Representative, their governor, and the federal government's Office of Indian Affairs Superintendent of Michigan, they used their annuity money to buy six sacred parcels of Indian Point land. Surely this meant, in their eyes, there would be no alienation from this land, forever. Using the specific wording "in trust to the Governor and his successors in office forever," did give them close to 50 years of idyllic life on the shore of Burt Lake.

Then, the seizure of their land and the Burn-Out of their village took place on October 15, 1900. Eleven long years later, the federal government's Department of Justice tried unsuccessfully to have the land returned to the Band. That was finally ruled unfavorably for the Band in May of 1917 after another six years.

Following this ruling by Judge Clarence Sessions to dismiss the Bill of Complaint against the McGinn estate, Michigan federal district Attorney John Kinnane wrote to Attorney General Thomas Watt Gregory about the case. His October 30, 1917, letter asked whether or not he should file an appeal before the time to do so would expire on December 22. It was later learned that Howell was adamant that an appeal be made, however, the Attorney General's office disagreed with him. It was the new Assistant Attorney General Leslie Garnett, who had been appointed to office in late 1917, and was not at all familiar with the case, who made the decision.

Garnett wrote a memorandum about the case, dated December 4, 1917.He expressed his opinion about why not to appeal the lawsuit. Once again, a federal official, without researching the actual facts, used the old Article Five misinterpretation. It began years after the 1855 Treaty of Detroit was negotiated and involved the treaty's language in its Article Five. Both the State of Michigan and federal officials failed to check the treaty journal notes to see the intent behind including Article Five's wording. It was simply an attempt to get rid of the notion that Anishinaabe Bands in Michigan belonged to either the Ottawa or the Chippewa Nation. That was never factual. The first instance of this inaccurate Article Five argument was in 1900 when the Secretary of the Interior used it as a basis for his statement, "It appears that this Band of Indians was never recognized as a Tribe or Nation, but is a small Band of Ottawa and Chippewa Indians in Michigan. The tribal relations of the Ottawa and Chippewa Indians of Michigan were dissolved by the Treaty of July 31, 1855. It would seem that they were relieved in whole from the guardianship and control of the United States. The government had no jurisdiction to sue on behalf of the Band to recover the lands."

Garnett goes on to opine the six land patents were granted "in fee simple" disregarding the "in trust to the Governor of Michigan" language. Thus, he wrongly contended, there were no restrictions against taxation.

Once again, ignorance of the facts played out against the Cheboiganing Band. Thus, they decided not to pursue their legitimate legal claim to their ancestral land. A letter was sent to Kinnane on December 8, 1917, by Frances J. Kearful, an Assistant Attorney General. It simply stated:
"Sir:
"You are informed after careful consideration it has been determined not to take an appeal in the case of the United States vs John McGinn, et al., in equity the United States Court for the Eastern District of Michigan."

That was it. Another government official's wrong interpretation of the facts and disregarding of Special Agent Joseph Howell's report in April of 1914 (a report of the actual facts in the case). However, the Cheboiganing Band members did not give up. They knew the truth and felt deeply the truth would prevail.

What is further disturbing of Judge Sessions' misinformed ruling is that once it was not appealed by the December 31, 1917, time limit, it could never be appealed. The legal principle of "res judicata" (Latin for a matter judged) means the case can never be re-litigated. Finality exists in Sessions' ruling.

Nothing was legal, whatsoever, about the Burn-Out at Indian Village. It was an incredibly cruel and intolerable act done with a bigoted mindset. Avarice and greed prevailed on that day. The immoral and illegal act was then justified by a series of egregious errors on behalf of local, state, and county officials whose job it was to avoid such errors. Malfeasance (a failure to perform one's duty) and misfeasance (willful failure to act), ignorance and prejudice allowed the atrocity to stand. The Department of Justice attorneys in Washington and Michigan did as thorough a job as they could. Clyde Webster devoted countless hours on behalf of the case. He and the department were up against strong odds in favor of "white wealth and status." Banker John McGinn wanted that valuable lakefront property and he got it. He only had a few years to possess it before passing away in January of 1912, not knowing whether or not his estate would be able to keep it.

Immediately following the 1917 verdict, Band elders Albert Shananquet and Enos Cabinaw continued to seek redress and restitution. In World War I, the Band had three of their members join the United States Army, just as their ancestors had done in the Civil War. During the 1920s,

Shananquet visited Washington, D.C., to advance the Band's cause. In 1934, Congress passed the Indian Reorganization Act meant to help the nation's Indigenous People suffering incredible economic hardship during those Great Depression years of the 1930s. The Band members signed a petition as required, asking the Office of Indian Affairs to grant them federal reaffirmation, something they had first obtained when their leader, Chief Chingassimo, signed the 1836 Treaty of Washington. It was ignored. The only Native American bands in Michigan that the federal government had granted recognition were those four bands who managed to maintain their ancestral land over the years. Those were the Saginaw and Chippewa Tribe in the lower peninsula and the Bay Mills Chippewa Indian Community, the Hannahville Indian Community, and the Keweenaw Bay Indian Community, all in the upper peninsula.

The Cheboiganing Band of Ottawa and Chippewa Indians found themselves in a federal government-imposed "Catch-22." Their federal recognition (actually reaffirmation) as a Michigan political and sovereign unit was denied because they had their ancestral land stolen from them in 1900. No ancestral land, no federal recognition, even though Congress had never voted to revoke that status as is required by law. It was an executive branch bureaucratic decision regarding the Band's federal status. That status meant the federal government would protect their lands and Band property, their sovereign status as a separate nation within this nation, and their long-held treaty negotiated the right to medical services in perpetuity. Now, the Band was told it did not have any of these, adding incredible insult to their 1900 injury.

In the 1940s, eight Band members joined this country's armed services, with two of them being killed in action. The Band joined the Michigan Ottawa Association in 1948, and, during that time, from the 1950s on, participated in Ghost Suppers to honor those who had "walked on" to heaven. Many members struggled economically, however, they held on to a belief that one day their Indian Village ancestral land would be back in their hands. They also kept in their memory the promise by the Michigan Legislature to provide them with 400 acres of state land somewhere in Cheboygan County — a choice of which they both agreed.

A strong concerted effort to regain those original 375 acres took place in the 1950s with the help of Band member Joseph Kishigo Jr. and the

Band's friend, Jonas Shawanesse, of Harbor Springs. Though their efforts were not successful, the Band continued to function. Weddings and funerals took place at the St. Mary's Catholic Church at Indianville, just north of the old Indian Village. Throughout the 1950s, Amos Shawa, an Elder, was considered the leader of the Band. Members attended Sunday church at St. Mary's throughout the 1950s and 1960s, having, in addition to the Ghost Suppers, Three Kings Suppers, square dances, quilting bees, wakes and quill box- and basket-making sessions.

By the 1960s, Edmund Parkey was the Band leader. Twenty-six burials at the St. Mary's Cemetery took place in the 1950s and ten more in the 1960s. The Band was as patient as Job, waiting for justice to take place on their Indian Point. Times were quite tough, and many Band members had to move to large cities to find work. Discrimination in the northland was still rampant, with "fish wars" breaking out during the 1970s and into the 1980s. Anishinaabe People had always been fishermen, and they remembered their 1836 Treaty rights. They had been promised on paper the right to hunt, gather, and fish in perpetuity as part of their negotiated settlement for their Michigan land. These sacred rights were under attack in the 1970s and finally settled in federal court in May of 1979.

Federal Judge for the Western District of Michigan Noel Fox issued a ruling allowing Native American commercial fishermen to continue fishing without any interference from the State of Michigan. During the trial, and after, northern Michigan saw the emergence of bumper stickers which read, "Save a Fish–Spear an Indian." It was a sentiment that had a long standing by some in the white community, a sentiment that had led to the 1900 Burn-Out, and was still strong 75 years later.

In October of 1977, Margaret Nongueskwa-Martell organized a meeting of Cheboiganing Band members in Lansing, Michigan. Later that month, the Band members met with the Native American Rights Fund at Lansing's Indian Center. They discussed any possible legal recourse to address the now 77-year-old theft of their ancestral land at Burt Lake. Two legal options were decided upon:

1. A lawsuit against the Governor of Michigan for breach of trustee responsibilities.

2. A lawsuit based on federal law to eject those who were presently living on the former Indian Village land.

In January of 1978, 27 descendants of the October 1900 Burn-Out signed a petition instructing the Native Rights Fund attorneys to file a lawsuit pertaining to the 375 lost acres of ancestral land. Some of the family names were Cabinaw, Shenoskey, Massey, Parkey, Shawandose and Shananquet. Meanwhile, during the 1970s, ten more burials took place at Indianville.

In July of 1980, Cheboiganing Band members incorporated as a non-profit 501(c)(3) organization under the name of the Burt Lake Band of Ottawa and Chippewa Indians. The Native Rights Fund sent then-Michigan Governor William Milliken a letter outlining the Band's priorities regarding their lost parcels of land. It states:

1. A strong desire of Elders to return to communal living in the proximity of the lands owned by their ancestors at Burt Lake
2. Development of congregate housing units for Elders
3. Fulfillment of the 1903 Joint Resolution No. 20 legislation calling for a 400-acre land restitution to the Cheboiganing Band

These goals are still priorities for the Band members in 2023. Ownership of ancestor's land is highly valued by Anishinaabe People. It is a way of preserving their cultural identity. It has both spiritual and cultural significance. Land is what their livelihood had been based on: hunting, gathering and agriculture.

In May of 1984, the State of Michigan granted the Burt Lake Band status as a Michigan Historic Indian Band. However, the Band's desire for reaffirmation by the federal government was still an issue. Since 1935, the Cheboiganing-Burt Lake Band had been seeking that reaffirmation first granted in 1836, and then arbitrarily withdrawn in 1935 by the Office of Indian Affairs, not by Congress. Reaffirmation meant medical care for the Elders. It meant economic development aid, federal government protection and free college tuition to Michigan colleges.

During the 1980s, 18 more burials took place at Indianville's Catholic cemetery. Finally, in June of 1993, a bill was introduced in Congress to reaffirm the Burt Lake Band of Ottawa and Chippewa, the Little Traverse Bands of Odawa and the Little River Bands of Ottawa, all of Michigan. By August, three separate bills were pending in the United States House of Representatives regarding reaffirmation for Michigan Indian Bands:

1. One to reaffirm the federal status of the Pokagon Band
2. One to reaffirm the federal status of the Little Traverse Bands of Odawa, and the Little River Band of Ottawa
3. One to reaffirm the federal status of the Burt Lake Band of Ottawa and Chippewa Indians

All of these four historic Bands of Michigan Indians were landless. All four bands supported each other, and had the written support of the other federally recognized, and/or, state-recognized bands. It was finally a time of excitement and jubilation for the Burt Lake Band members who had waited so long for this partial redress of their grievances. It was a step they hoped would eventually result in their regaining the Burt Lake ancestral land or the state granting of the 1903 promised 400 acres of their choice.

Luckless fate once again intervened against the Burt Lake Band. Just as the ill-fated choice of federal Judge Sessions in the 1911 Justice Department lawsuit had doomed the chance of land restitution for the Band, the same type of fate struck again on August 3, 1994, in the House of Representatives Washington, D.C. This time it doomed the reaffirmation of the Band by the federal government. On that day, in the House of Representatives, the Burt Lake Band, the Little Traverse Band, the Little River Band and the Pokagon Band of Potawatomi were all to be voted on for reaffirmation by the Representatives. The approved bills would then go over to the Senate for a vote. It was all set with Representative Bart Stupak helping lead the way. At the last minute a couple of Representatives from other states raised an objection to the Burt Lake Band on the grounds that they had been added as a rider to the original bill for the Little Traverse and Little River Bands. That had been done because all three Bands had identical historical and fact patterns (except, the Burt Lake Band had their ancestral land illegally stolen).

The opposing Representatives wanted the Burt Lake Band to first have a hearing before the Natural Resources Committee. It was too late in the 103rd Congressional Session to hold one. So, at the very last minute, for the Little Traverse and Little River Bands to be approved, Burt Lake Band members who were in Washington to witness the passage of the bill, instead agreed to withdraw their Band from the bill. They were promised that they would then be reaffirmed in the new session of Congress beginning in January of 1995. However, as with the quirk of fate in 1911 with Judge Sessions, the November 1994 election put Newt Gingrich and the Republican Party in charge of the House of Representatives. He, and they, wanted nothing to do with Congress granting the Band reaffirmation.

Disappointment and determination were the mantra of the Burt Lake Band. Members, believing they had finally achieved one of their main goals, reaffirmation, now had to rethink their strategy. Instead of Congressional approval, the Band now hoped the Bureau of Indian Affairs would finally act on their 1985 Petition for Federal Recognition sent to the Bureau in September of 1985, now some ten years earlier. Finally, in 1998, the Bureau sent a letter to the Band stating their Petition for Reaffirmation was finally under "active review." Meanwhile, during the 1990s, 20 more burials took place at the Indianville cemetery.

On March 30, 2001, now over 100 years since the loss of their Indian Village land, the Burt Lake Band had a federal lawsuit initiated in Washington, D.C., against the Secretary of the Interior Gale Norton (who oversaw the Bureau of Indian Affairs). The Band's legal action sought an injunction by the deferral court that would place the Burt Lake Band on the Department of Interior's Federal List of Acknowledged Indian Tribes. The Band asked for a declaratory judgment that, officially, the Band had never been legally terminated by a Congressional Act. By then, some of the Band's members had been invited to join the Little Traverse Bay Bands of Odawa, and after doing so, received medical services and other benefits. Others were adamant about staying in the Burt Lake Band, of which their ancestors had been born and raised. A federal judge in August of 2002 dismissed the suit on the grounds the Band had not exhausted all administrative remedies it could use.

Again, time passed, and finally, in September of 2006, the Bureau of Indian Affairs, 20 years after receiving the Burt Lake Band petition for reaffirmation, ruled the Band did not qualify due to it not meeting certain criteria for acknowledgment. The bureau basically took the position that the Band had not maintained itself as a political unit since 1900. That meant the bureaucrats at the Bureau of Indian Affairs felt no authority or political influence over Band members had been maintained by any leader. Of course, those in the Band highly disagreed.

With continued patience and hope, the Band asked Representative

Bart Stupak, whose Congressional district contained the Burt Lake Band's Brutus, Michigan, office, to introduce legislation in the United States House of Representatives "to reaffirm and clarify the Federal relationship of the Burt Lake Band as a distinct federally recognized Indian Tribe" (September 19, 2007). President George W. Bush's Acting Deputy Assistant of Indian Affairs testified against the bill, and it lingered in the House with no action taken. Meanwhile, between the year 2000 and 2009, ten more burials took place at Indianville.

Leadership of the Band was assumed by Bruce Hamlin in 2011. Hamlin is the descendant of Moses Hamlin, who was an Elder at Indian Village on the day of the Burn-Out. Another ancestor of Bruce Hamlin was Michilimackinac Ottawa Chief Minavavana, who was quoted at Fort Michilimackinac in 1761 as stating, "Englishmen! Although you have conquered the French, you have not yet conquered us! We are not your slaves. These lakes, these woods and mountains, were left to us by our ancestors. They are our inheritance, and we will part with them to none." (recorded by Alexander Henry)

Band chairperson Hamlin and the Band Council continued the long effort for reaffirmation and ancestral land in Cheboygan County. In 2016, the Band engaged the legal services of former congressman Stupak, a member of the Washington, D.C., law firm Venable. Venable had a long history of pro bono work for clients with economic difficulties, and Stupak had deep knowledge of the Band's plight.

On January 9, 2017, a lawsuit was filed in federal court in Washington, D.C., against the Interior Department of the United States and its Bureau of Indian Affairs.

This lawsuit was filed 105 years after the June 1917 lawsuit brought against John McGinn in Michigan's federal court. The Band's persistence and patience of Job was rewarded by Stupak and his law firm taking the case on their behalf, just as the Justice Department had done in 1911. The suit contended that the Bureau of Indian Affairs "non-decision" regarding the Band's petition for reaffirmation was discriminatory and precluded the Burt Lake Band from receiving necessary benefits and services, such as access to education, health, and welfare programs available only to members of recognized Indian Bands or Tribes.

The 2017 lawsuit's introduction stated:

"After nearly 200 years of mistreatment, Plaintiff Burt Lake Band of

Ottawa and Chippewa Indians ("the Band") submits this motion for summary judgment on Counts IV, V, and VI of the Complaint as part of its longstanding efforts to obtain recognition and fair and equitable treatment from the federal government. Without any statutory authority, the Department of the Interior, through the Bureau of Indian Affairs ("BIA"), unlawfully adopted a regulation, 25 C.F.R. §83.4(d), that created an absolute prohibition on the Band's ability to submit additional evidence in support of its application for federal recognition as a sovereign Indian tribe. In doing so, Defendants have denied the Band the right to petition for federal acknowledgment as a sovereign tribe and for redress of grievances under the First Amendment, on the sole ground that its initial petition was previously denied. Additionally, the regulation is arbitrary and capricious because it denies the Band and other tribes the right to petition the government for statutory rights based solely on the administrative convenience of the BIA."

It has now been 123 years since the Burt Lake Band first suffered the loss of their ancestral land, the aftermath of which, left them not only landless, but as a result of their land being stolen, has left them without recognition by the federal government as a sovereign Band with treaty rights that first began in March of 1836. Through sheer tenacity, patience and moral strength, the Band has maintained its quest to regain their land and rightful recognition. Their quest for justice continues.

who?

Who owned the lands where
America stands
When the White Man crosses
the sea?
Whose word was good on his
own feet stood,
The freest of the free?
The Indian

Who had naught of guile, and for
a long while
Thought the White Man as
honest as he?
Who found, too late, it was sad
fate
The dupe of the strangers, to be.
The Indian

Who, knowing not, worth of
things he got,
His birth-right traded for trash?
While the lands he sold, worth
thousands in gold.
The buyers soon turned into
cash?
The Indian

When the Pilgrims set foot on
that "Rock Island Coast,"
Who gave them a welcoming
hand,
Went into the forest to get them
meat,
And helped to clear the land?
The Indian

Who signed treaties in all good
faith,
First by the Whites to be broken?
The Indian

Who was it had the "crooked
tongue,"
By whom the crooked word
spoken?
The Whites

"Civilized" People to the lands,
That people not "civilized" had
For "Christians" to take from the
"savages,"
In their eyes was good, not bad,

The "March of Progress" made
the excuse
For taking over their lands,
And, perhaps, it was inevitable,
They should suffer these wrongs
at our hands.

But, while we, who now live,
were not to blame,
Should feel the blush of shame,
That the treatment given the
Indians,
Left a blot on America's name.

Author unknown

acknowledgments

First, a very special thanks to the Burt Lake Band of Ottawa & Chippewa Indians who entrusted me to write this story. It has been brewing in the back of my mind for 50 years since first learning about the sordid event. This story would not have been printed without the help of Charles L. Wilson, III, a friend of the Band, and his connection to the Henry E. and Consuelo S. Wenger Foundation.

Dr. Dennis Albert, PhD, University of Michigan Bio-Station ecology lecturer and research faculty member at Oregon State University (Horticulture) and Central Michigan University (Biology), contributed to this effort. Dr. Alice Littlefield, Central Michigan University professor of Anthropology-Sociology Emeritus, a long-time friend of the Burt Lake Band, was very helpful. Wayne Richard Smith, Michigan attorney Emeritus and friend, was also a part of this process.

Thank you to Greenwood Cemetery for providing a robust archive on its website, www.gwood.us. This site was vital in my research for this and other historical writings.

Petoskey author and literary critic Glen Young, owner of Bear River Literary, began the editing portion of this story. Deborah Richmond, a Burt Lake Band member and owner of Tekkbuzz.com, was very important to the final editing process.

Renée Tanner, a graphic designer, was the force behind the cover and the book design. Traverse City author Mardi Link's contribution set the tone for the book.

A special thanks to former Congressman Bart Stupak and now Burt Lake Band attorney with the Venable Group in Washington, D.C. He has been a Burt Lake Band advocate for over 30 years and is currently helping the Band's effort to be reaffirmed by the United States federal government.

A thank you to Harbor Springs author Kristie Dickinson for her technical assistance. Dr. Margaret Noodin, poet and co-editor of Ojibwe.net, was the translator for the Anishinaabemowin words. Finally, my wife, Margaret "Maggie" Daniels read every word of the rough draft, as she has done with all of my stories. Thank you all!

— Richard A. Wiles

sources

A Bitter Memory: Seeking "Maamaw Gwayak" (Social Justice) at Burt Lake, Richard A. Wiles, The Michigan Historical Review, Spring 2016, Central Michigan University

"An Ethnohistorical Report on the Burt Lake Band of Ottawa and Chippewa Indians (aka The Cheboiganing Band of Indians), Dr. George Cornell, Michigan State University, 1994

Atlas of Great Lakes Indian History, Dr. Helen H. Tanner, University of Oklahoma Press, 1986

Diary, Father Francis Pierz, missionary, Minnesota Historical Society-http:// collections.mnhs.org › articles

Disinherited: The Lost Birthright of the American Indian, Dale Van Every, 1966, William Morrow & Company, New York

"LO, THE POOR INDIAN": NATIVE AMERICANS, REALITY AND IMAGERY

Reviewed Work: Indian Work: Language and Livelihood in Native American History by Daniel H. Usner, Jr., Reviews in American History Vol. 38, No. 3 (September 2010), pp. 407-413, John Hopkins University Press

Michigan Alumnus, Volume 12, 1905

Rites of Conquest: The History and Culture of Michigan's Native Americans, Dr. Charles Cleland, University of Michigan Press, Ann Arbor, Michigan, 1992

"The Burt Lake Band: An Historical Report on the Trust Lands of Indian Village," Dr. Richard White, Michigan State University, 1978

The centennial history of Cheboygan County and village [electronic resource]: organization of the county, townships and village, early history, settlements, improvements, present business, valuable statistical tables, advertisements. Supplement, descriptive of Mackinac Island, W. H. Ware, Northern Tribune Print, Cheboygan, Michigan, 1876

The Fire Not Forgotten, Traverse the Magazine, March 4, 2008

The "Odious Tax Title": A study in Nineteenth Century Legal History, Robert P. Swierenga, The American Journal of Legal History, Oxford University Press, 1971

"The Natural Ecology and Cultural History of the Colonial Point Red Oak Stands," Technical Report No. 14, Dr. Dennis Albert, Dr. Leah Minc, University of Michigan Biological Station, March 1987

photo usage

ON THE COVER: The Indian Village at Burt Lake in 1890. Public Domain. Cloud added from Adobe Stock.

Indian Village Life: Photos from the archives of the Burt Lake Band of Ottawa and Chippewa Indians used with permission.

Chief Red Cloud: "Red Cloud," black and white photograph by the American photographer John K. Hillers (1843-1925), published by Charles M. Bell. The portrait of the chief of the Oglala Lakota Sioux was taken at Washington, D.C., circa 1880. Public Domain.

Cloud: Adobe Stock.

John McGinn: Photo of John W. McGinn headstone in Cheboygan County's Pine Hill Cemetery courtesy of a user of findagrave.com and used with permission.

Fred Ming: Michigan House Speaker portrait 1933. Public Domain.

Good Samaritan: The Good Samaritan tending the wounds of the traveler (Luke 10:25-37) painting by Nicolaas Roosendael. Public Domain.

Lo the Poor Indian: Smithsonian Institute. Harry T. Peters, America on Stone Lithography Collection 1875. Public Domain.

Federal Government 1911 Circuit Court document: National Archives

Judge C.W. Sessions: U.S. Library of Congress Prints and Photographs division. No known copyright restrictions.

Federal Court building, Bay City: Used with permission from the Court Historical Society for the United States District Court for the Eastern District of Michigan

Verdict and its Aftermath: Photos of Albert Shananquet from the Oct. 1, 1958, issue of the Straitsland Resorter. Printed with permission from its owner at the time of this publication.

"Scrapbook photos" from the center of the book are all from Burt Lake Band archives and used with permission. The treaty image in the center is from the author.

Members of the Burt Lake Band participate in 2015's Walk of Remembrance, a journey the group travels every fall from the site of the old Indian Village heading north three miles to Indianville.

Made in the USA
Columbia, SC
02 February 2025

53191773R00067